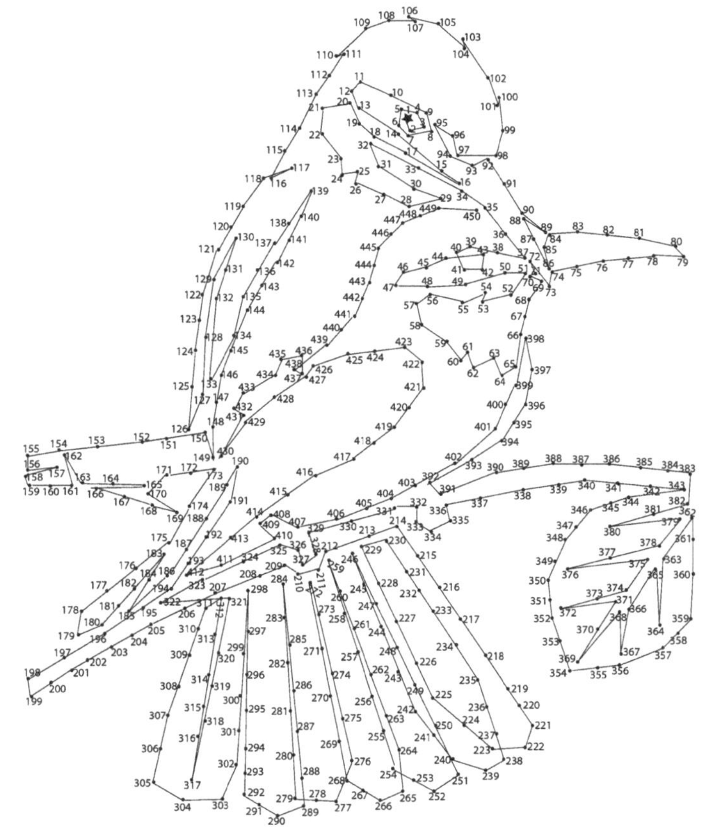

Big Book of Large Print Animals
Dot-to-Dot Puzzles from 300 to 615 Dots

By Dottie's Crazy Dot-to-Dots

WELCOME!

We invite you to relax with the beautiful images

found in these pages whether this is your first

or 100th dot to dot book.

The directions are simple: Start with dot #1,

and draw a line to dot #2, then a line from dot #2

to dot #3, and so on. A picture will appear

as you connect the dots.

Take all the time you need and don't worry,

you will always find the next dot,

even if you don't see it at first.

We hope you enjoy this

super challenging dot to dot book.

320 319 33 34 55 32 35 54 53 56
321 318 31 36
322 317 30 37 52 57
323 39
324 316 38 41
325 40 58
326 315 50 59
327 29 43 48
314 42 49
328 44 46 60
329 312 313 25 28 45 47 61
311 24 26
310 22 23 6 5 15 27 62
21 10 7 9 4 16 63
309 11 1 8 3 17
308 12 2 14
20 13 18
76 19 64
307 75
303 77 65
302 306 66 92
301 73 74 93
304 305 72 78 69 68 67 94
300 71 91
299 298 70 79 86 89 90 95
297 81 80 82 84 85 87 88 97 96
296 295 83 98
294
293 100 99
292
291 290
289 287 185 102 101
288 104 103
286 184 116
285 187 183
284 186 105
283 282 182 115 107 106 128 138
188 108
281 209 181 159 114
230 280 117 109 134
279 208 210 189 190 180 158 112 113 127
229 206 191 157 110 125 129 133 139
277 207 204 179 160 155 131 135
278 231 228 276 205 192 161 156 154 118 111 137
235 220 194 162 123
259 252 244 239 232 224 211 193 178 163 153 152 121
260 241 234 227 221 274 203 195 177 165 164 119 126 130
258 247 255 243 236 230 225 217 215 213 202 200 198 196 151 149 147 143 124 132
261 246 240 238 223 219 214 201 197 176 170 167 145 122 120 136
257 253 248 245 235 273 212 174 172 166 150 148 146 144 142 141 140
262 256 249 240 231 228 276 205 233 237
263 254 242 226 222 218 216 199 175 173 171 169 168
264 250 251 268 269 270 271 272
265 266 267

285 287 290 293 288 291 294

283 284 286 289 292 295 297

281 282 327 325 323 296 298 299

280 279 329 328 326 324 322 300 301 303

278 331 330 321 319 302 305

277 276 333 332 320 304 307

275 271 270 334 318 316 306 317 315 308 309

273 269 268 337 335 267 336

274 272 265 266 310 313 314

263 264 339 338 219 217 64 63 51 52

261 340 221 218 216 70 65 62 312 311 56 53 55 50

259 262 223 341 225 224 222 220 199 200 71 69 66 59 61 57 58 54 49

257 260 258 227 226 197 198 68 72 60 9 8 47 48 46 43 42

256 229 196 201 215 67 3 4 5 7 44 39 45 38 41 40 36

255 228 195 202 10 2 1 6 12 33 37 34 35 84

254 230 194 193 73 11 32 17 31 83

231 192 157 203 214 74 22 21 13

252 253 233 156 204 213 75 23 14 16 30 82 85

250 251 232 191 159 158 160 155 212 76 24 20 26 15 29 28 81 87

234 190 189 161 205 25 27 80 77 78 79 86 88

249 154 206 211 210 92 90 104 105

236 162 152 153 207 208 209 93 91 96 103

247 248 235 186 151 149 97 94 102 106

237 187 163 150 148 147 99 100 98 101 108

245 246 238 185 184 164 143 146 145 107

244 165 142 144 110 109

243 239 183 182 166 139 140 112 111

241 242 181 179 137 138

240 180 167 136 119 117 115 113

178 176 174 168 135 120 118 116 114 122

177 175 173 171 169 134 127 126 121 123

172 170 133 128 129 125 124

132 131 130

79 80 81
78 49 47 82
77 48
76 51 98 83
65 53 9 50 39 40 84
52 10 46 38 97 99
66 64 5 8 31 32 41 85
75 54 4 1 7 45 37 36 33
11 3 2 14 30 35 34 96 100 86
63 43
74 67 55 12

73 13 15 28 44 95 87
62 56 17 16 29 101
68 27
61 18 26 88
57 94 102
72 60 108 19 25
20 24 89 341
71 69 58 107 21 22 23 103 200 340
70 59 109 211 106 105 104 208 93 92 91 90 201 199 339
210 209 207 204 234
110 212 206 205 203 233 198 338
111 213 202 337
112 214 232 196 235
113 215 226 231 197 236 336
114 216 335
115 217 225 227 230 195 334
116 218 220 224 228 229 237
117 219 239 238 333
118 221 222 194 332
150 223 161 193 240 242 331
119 151 149 241 244 243 330
152 148 192 245 329
120 153 162 160 191 247 246
147 154 190 251 252 328
121 155 189 250 253 254 255 326
122 156 157 159 188 249 272 256 327
158 163 273 257 325
146 164 187 271 258
123 165 186 274 269 261 260 324
124 145 185 275 270 268 259 323
144 166 276 267 262
126 143 284 283 263
127 167 184 285 282 277 266 322 306
141 142 286 265 264 305 307
128 172 173 287 281 280 279 278 321 304
129 171 168 291 296 303 308
130 138 170 174 183 289 290 292 297 301 302 320 309
134 133 140 175 179 288 293 295 299 300 319
31 180 181 182 294 298 316 317 318 311 310
132 135 136 137 177 178 315 314 313 312

341 340 342 343 344
339 4 13 14 15
338 5 3 10 11 16 18
6 1 9 12 17
7 8 2 20 19 22 23 21 24
337 336 32 31 30 28 27 26 25
335 334 36 34 33 29 48 51 49 50
37 35 52 54
333 38 40 42 44 46 53
332 39 41 43 45 47 55 56 94
331 298 297 127 128 95 66 57
330 299 296 126 125 65
329 300 124 93 67 58
301 302 295 129 96 69 64 68
328 303 123 122 59
327 130 131 120 121 92 63
294 97 98 71 70 60
326 304 118 119 99 62
325 317 293 91
324 318 305 132 133 134 117 100 101 61 72
323 319 306 292 115 116 102 103 104 105 73 90 75
322 315 307 291 135 114 106 107 74 76 77 89 78 86 85 168
320 311 308 321 310 290 289 138 136 112 113 110 108 87 81 79 80 83 84 180 169
314 288 139 140 137 111 109 144 164 167 82 181 182 185 186
313 312 287 141 142 143 146 147 145 163 165 166 170 171 172 173 174 175 176 177 178 179 183 184
309 152 151 149 148 150 162 153 161 160 159 154 155 158
156 157 286 235 234 231 230 228 229
283 284 285 236 237 233 232 227 226 238 239 224 225 223 222 221 220 219 218 217
280 281 282 243 242 241 240 205 206 207 203 202 200 198 196 195 194 193 192 190 191 188 189 187
278 277 276 275 274 244 251 254 255 256 257 258 264 208 209 210 201 212 211 213 199 214 215 216
279 245 252 253 250 246 249 260 259 261 262 263 267 265 266 268 269 270 271 272 273

328 327 329 326
332 331 330
325 324 17 18 50 51 52 53
323 333 16 10 11 5 6 19 49 47 46 45 54
322 321 15 4 2 7 12 48 36 37 38 44 55 56
315 316 334 9 3 8 27 35 39 43 57 61
317 14 13 20 42 58 59 62
318 320 60 64 63
314 319 311 335 21 22 34 345 344 65
313 312 23 32 343
309 310 336 25 24 31 26 27 30 28 66 67
337 338 339 340 29 342 68 70 341 69 71
308 72 75
248 247 244 73 77 76
307 306 249 246 245 243 189 187 79 78
242 241 188 81 80
305 250 240 239 190 186
238 237 192 184 185 82
193 191
251 217 182 180 183 84 83
304 303 219 194 181
235 218 196 179 177 85
252 236 220 215 195 178
233 221 223 216 197 199 201 86 87
302 231 232 234 214 198 200 202 176 88 105 104 103
300 253 230 229 228 222 224 212 213 204 203 174 106 89 90
301 299 227 205 175 107 91
287 286 254 226 225 211 210 209 206 173 168 167
298 255 208 207 172 171 169 170 166 108 102
297 256 258 162 165 164 92
284 285 257 264 259 134 163 109
288 267 283 263 160 161 101
296 282 135 137 157 152 155 110
294 295 281 276 266 262 265 261 260 136 159 158 153 148 154 151 111 93
289 268 280 132 138 147 139 146 149 150 121 116 94 95 100
275 277 279 133 131 140 141 144 143 145 115 114 113 112 96
293 292 270 273 274 278 130 129 128 127 142 120 117 97 98
291 269 126 119 118 99
290 271 272 125 124 123

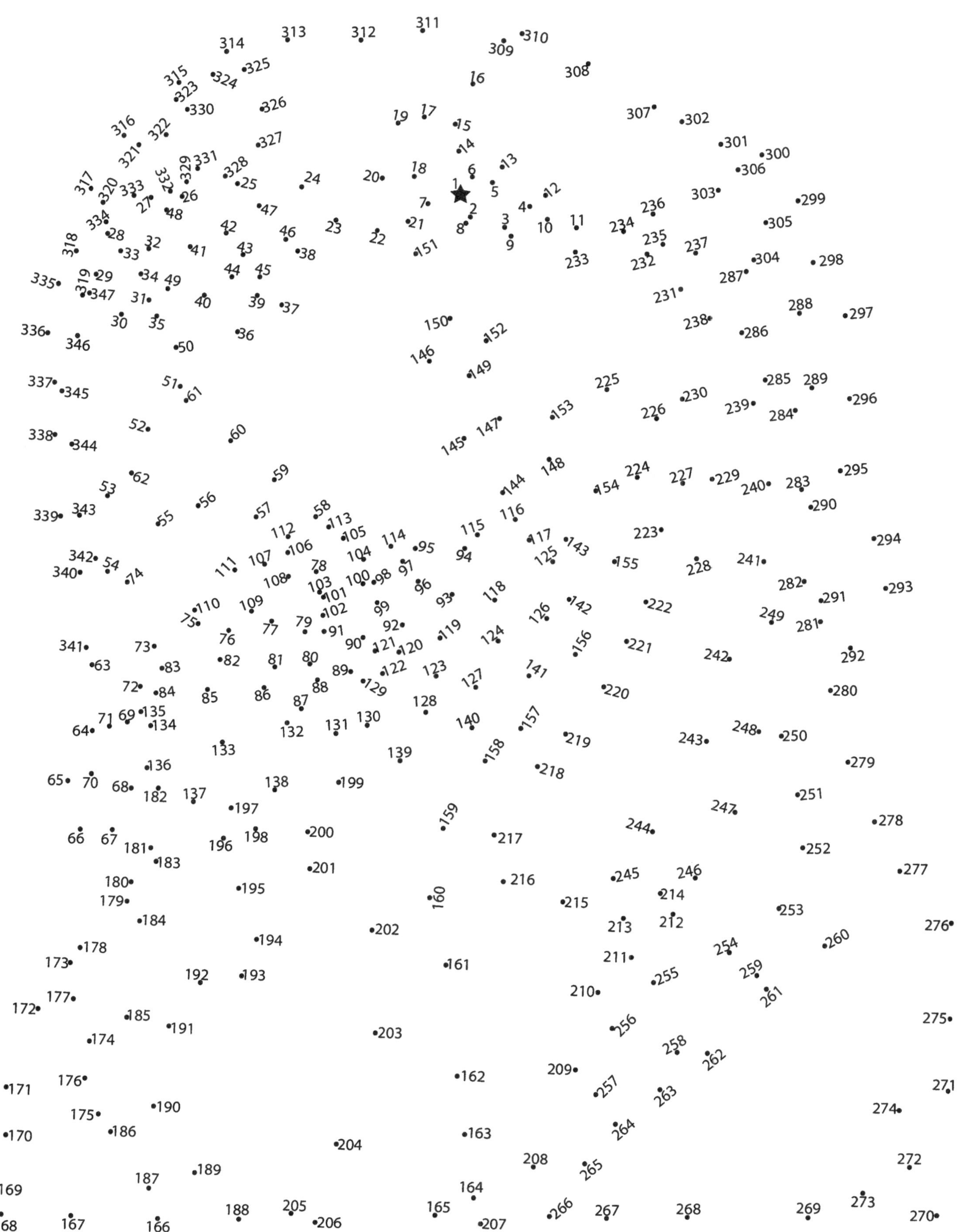

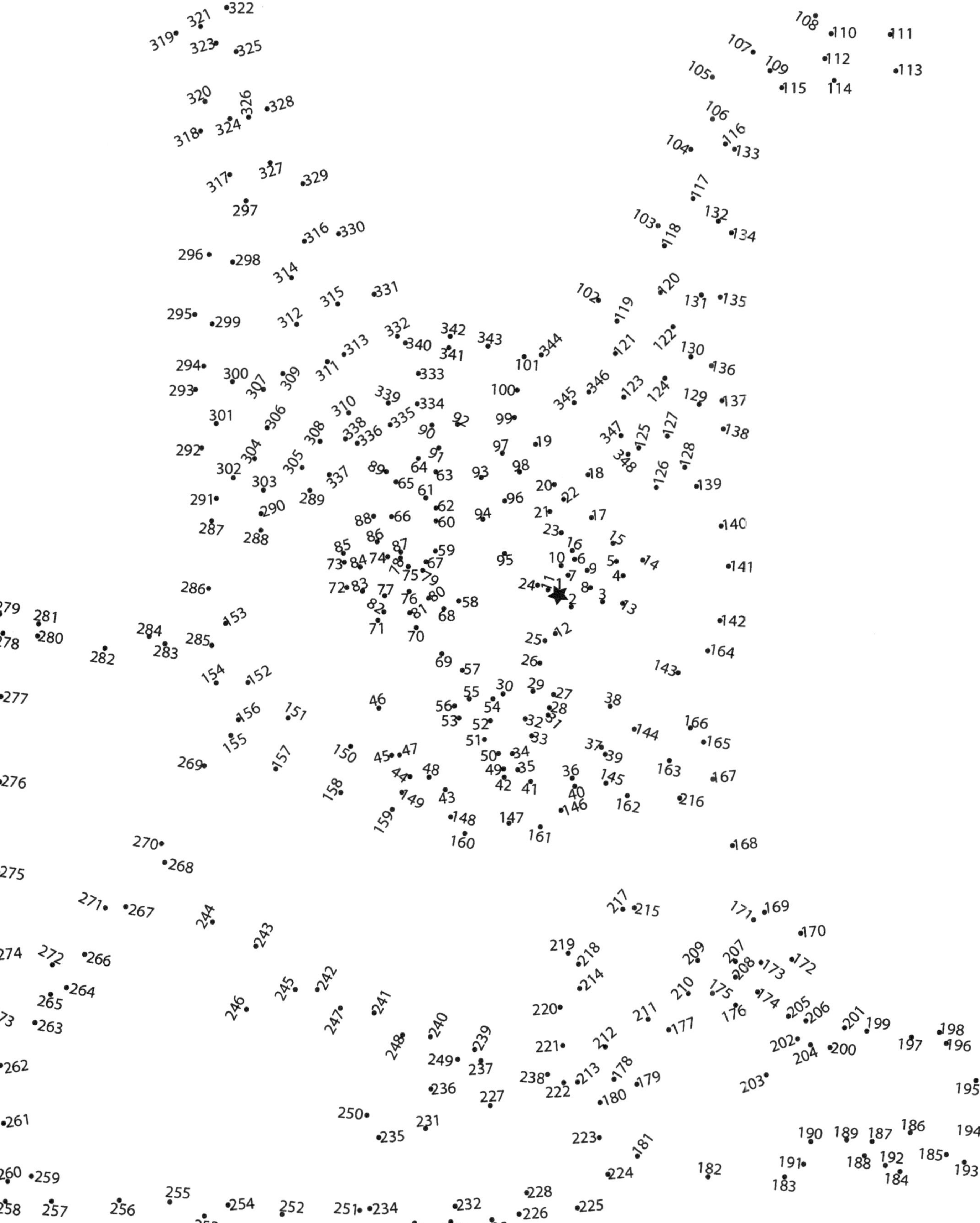

94 95 84 93 96 106 107 105 108 109 120
83 85 91 92 97 98 99 100 102 104 110 111 119 121
82 87 89 90 101 103 113 116 118 122 112
86 88 54 55 115 117 123 114
81 47 48 53 56 57 124
80 45 46 49 51 58 125 126 59 128 127
44 43 34 30 74 3 61 60
78 77 42 35 31 33 29 50 52 8 5 6 2 130 129 215
79 41 36 32 37 38 28 9 1 62 63 132 131 213 216
178 75 40 39 64 133 214
179 176 74 73 27 10 134 212 218 217
177 174 172 72 19 65 135 136 210
181 171 71 26 17 20 11 138 137 220 226
180 183 173 170 25 16 21 12 66 139 211 219
182 168 167 70 24 22 15 67 142 141 140 209 221 225 227
312 184 186 169 166 164 163 159 23 14 68 155 151 147 143 207
185 162 160 156 152 150 146 144 208
311 188 165 158 154 148 206 222 224 229
313 187 309 189 161 157 149 145 204 205 251 228
314 310 191 190 192 194 153 202 203 223 250 230
315 317 308 193 195 197 199 201 278 252 249 232
316 286 196 200 198 277 231 233
318 307 287 283 281 279 253 248 247
338 340 344 345 347 319 320 285 284 282 280 254 246 234
339 341 342 343 346 348 321 276 245 236
337 322 323 306 288 235
336 324 326 305 289 275 255 237
325 327 328 243 244 239
335 272 271 274 270 238 240
334 333 332 331 330 329 304 290 273 256 242 241
303 299 294 295 291 269 265 261 257
302 298 300 293 292 266 260 262 258
301 297 296 268 267 264 263 259

239 234 235 233 236 232 237 238 240 231

244 243 242 241 245 247 246 248

162 283 282 281 276 275 267 266 258 256 251 257 250 249 230

158 159 160 161 284 163 279 280 277 278 273 274 268 264 265 259 255 252 181 182 183 175 174

155 157 156 154 153 152 285 164 272 270 269 263 260 254 253 179 177 180 176

149 151 150 286 165 271 167 166 262 261 168 169 178 170 171 172 173 184 229

146 148 147 144 145 143 287 288 289 291 185 292 296 187 186 188 189 190 228

141 142 140 290 293 294 297 298 299 300 227

138 139 137 136 135 134 132 321 319 320 322 323 318 317 309 307 305 295 306 304 308 315 316 310 311 302 303 301 191 192 226 193 195 197 225 224 198

133 130 131 129 125 92 91 87 90 71 72 70 69 73 74 68 66 65 63 62 61 60

128 126 124 86 84 93 85 83 81 89 88 79 80 78 77 76 75 33 35 34 32 31 30 64 67 37 36 40 41 28 29 24 23 22 59 342 341 332 330 329 194 196 331 333 340 338 334 335 339 336 337 345 346 347 349 348 344 353 355 354 356 350 351 352

94 96 95 97 98 44 45 38 39 42 26 16 27 25 17 18 19 21 20 57 58

127 121 122 117 118 100 99 101 48 46 47 7 8 5 4 1 2 3 15 14 56 55 205 201 202 204 206 207 212 208 213 209 211 210 216 214 218 215 219 221 222 223 220 217 115 116 113 119 114 112 111 110 109 108 106 107 102 103 105 104 51 53 52 50 49 11 9 10 12 13 54 199 200 203 198 224

60 61 74 59 62 75 40 39 63 73 48 41 38 58 64 66 76 49 47 57 65 72 37 56 68 77 50 42 44 36 54 55 67 71 46 35 43 34 53 7 8 69 45 16 6 5 9 78 51 52 33 1 10 70 32 15 2 4 79 17 14 3 11 31 12 352 24 18 80 30 25 22 362 13 353 351 26 21 361 81 29 20 354 27 360 350 28 359 355 82 358 356 347 348 349 357 346 83 345 167 166 344 343 342 85 84 341 168 164 165 86 163 340 339 116 87 338 169 170 135 117 114 115 171 173 162 136 133 131 112 89 88 337 336 172 160 137 134 132 118 113 90 237 174 159 161 120 111 91 335 236 139 138 129 130 119 298 234 235 140 158 128 121 110 92 334 175 177 123 109 332 297 233 176 141 127 126 122 108 93 333 231 232 178 157 124 107 94 296 299 295 239 142 125 331 230 179 180 156 143 106 95 325 181 155 96 324 330 294 300 272 270 228 229 218 216 144 105 103 329 326 271 240 227 217 151 146 101 99 323 328 306 293 292 269 225 215 182 154 148 145 104 97 327 290 219 153 150 147 102 100 98 322 305 291 241 226 152 149 307 304 303 289 273 242 224 214 183 302 268 220 321 320 301 223 308 274 243 184 319 267 222 213 185 318 317 310 288 275 266 221 316 311 244 186 312 287 276 212 211 187 315 313 286 277 245 210 188 189 190 191 192 206 193 195 314 285 278 265 246 209 208 207 204 205 194 196 264 263 247 202 203 201 200 198 197 262 248 249 250 199 284 283 279 282 280 281 258 261 259 260 254 251 257 256 255 253 252

66
67 74
65
52 53 54 75 76 68 64
51 44 43 55 77 69 63
49 50 11 10 9 78
48 46 45 12 3 2 1 8 21 42 79
47 44 13 4 20 22 41 56 81 73 70 62
15 17 5 6 19 23 40 39 83 80
30 28 16 18 24 57
29 25 82 71 61
27 26 38 58 84 72 60
31 34 35 37 59
32 33 36
362
361
360 85
87 86
359 88
358
356
357 355
354 91 89
90
353 92
93
352
94
350 95 101 102
351 96 100 103 112 111 113
104 108 109 110 114 139
349 97 99 118 117 115
348 105 106 107 122 119 116 135 140
126 123 121 120 138 141
334 125 124 131 165
98 130 132 133 134 136 137 142
347 127 149 145 144 143 164 166
345 342 335 333 318 128 129 146 161 162 163 167 185
346 264 153 152 148 147 160 169 168 184 218 186
341 317 265 258 150 151 157 158 159 173 170 219
332 263 155 156 176 174 172 171 183 189 187
344 340 343 336 319 304 257 259 253 175 180 181 182 189 188 217 220
305 303 262 261 260 256 252 254 248 201 177 178 179 193 190 213 216
331 320 306 316 266 270 255 251 200 202 196 195 194 192 191 214 215
339 337 330 312 311 302 300 273 249 244 199 198 203 208 212 221 223
338 329 321 315 301 267 250 247 243 241 204 209 207 211 222 224
325 322 313 299 268 269 271 272 274 245 242 240 235 205 206 210 228
307 310 298 295 292 275 277 280 283 232 227 225
328 289 239 236 226
314 286 278 279 281 229
327 326 324 323 308 309 296 293 290 288 287 285 284 282 238 237 234 233 231 230
297 294 291

370 371 369 368 367 366 365 372 373 364 363 362 361 360 359 357 353 356 355 353 354 352
374 51 52 50 53 49 54 48 55 56
375 380 381 42 43
379 40 41 35 36 37 44
376 5 6 39 38 229
378 4 1 3 2 7 228 230 351
377 8 45 47 254 255 349 350
9 6 15 14 31 46 58 227 231 253 256 258 348
10 13 30 57 226 232 252 257 259 347
17 11 12 20 175 224 225 233 251 250 260 346 345
18 19 21 29 59 174 223 235 234 305 344
22 23 24 26 28 60 173 176 170 249 261 303 342 343
25 27 62 177 248 247 304 340
61 63 172 171 65 169 168 181 183 185 222 236 246 262 302 306 341 339
64 178 179 180 184 186 221 220 237 264 263 300 301 307 338
66 67 68 166 167 190 182 188 187 219 218 239 245 265 309 308 297 310
69 71 70 165 191 189 217 238 241 242 243 244 298 299 337
73 72 164 193 215 216 240 266 295 296 335 336
74 76 75 163 192 214 212 268 267 311 334
78 77 195 194 213 211 269 313 312 314 330 332
80 79 162 196 210 271 288 290 292 294 333
81 83 161 160 197 209 270 272 287 289 291 293 283 281 280 315 329 328 327 331 324 323
82 84 85 159 198 208 205 206 204 207 203 273 286 285 284 282 279 316 317 319 326 325 322
86 87 88 89 158 157 199 200 201 202 98 274 275 276 277 278 318 320 321
154 155 156 90 97 96 99 115 116 120 121 122
153 148 147 91 92 100 101 103 114 117 118 119
152 146 140 94 95 102 113 112 123
151 149 93 104 107 106 108 111 124
145 141 142 143 139 138 137 136 105 135 109 110
150 144 131 132 130 133 134 129 128 127 126 125

373 374
371 372 390 391 385 375
370 389 393 397 386 384
388 392 387 383 382 376
380 381 378 377
369 379 3 4
368 2 5
367 1
366 6
330
7
331 365 8 12 13
332 14
9
324 333 355 11
334 364 18
10 17 15
335 354 356 363 22 21 19
337 336 338 20 35 16 36
341 339 353 362 23
357 24 31 34 37
282 317 342 25 28 30
302 304 315 27 32 33 84
316 343 340 352 29 85 83
303 361 91 26 82 71
281 305 93 86 81 38
273 358 90 87 72
272 314 344 360 94 92 80 73
280 306 345 351 95 89 74 39
271 313 346 350 359 240 96 88 75 70
279 274 347 79 76 40
270 311 97 77 202 203 205 69
278 307 312 310 348 349 78 201 41
269 277 241 98 199 68 67 66
268 259 275 308 309 242 239 198 64 59 60 65 50 45 42
267 252 276 243 99 195 197 63 58 54 55 44 43
264 258 253 246 238 61 49 51 47
260 257 250 245 244 204 62 53 46
266 263 254 247 206 57 56 52 48
265 262 248 200 188 187 186
261 249 237
153 152 151 148 147 193 194 196 207
154 150 236 100 192 190 185
155 144 149 101 191 210 209
143 136 146 235 232 231 102 103 189 211
137 145 134 233 230 220 216 104
156 135 229 224 219 214 217 212 208
142 133 228 223 218 221 213 184
157 138 132 234 227 226 222 105 178 179 183
122 123 108 109 107 106 177 180 181 182 174
121 110 111 112 176 175
158 131 124
141 139 130 120 119
140 118 117 116 113 167
159 129 128 127 126 125 115 114 168 166 173
160 161 162 163 164 169 165 170 171 172

324 326 328 327 329 331
322 323 325 360 359 327 353 330
366 365 352 332
361 358 354 334
364 355 343 333
362 350 345 340 341 336 338 335
357 349 339 385 386 184 337 185 170 192
363 356 348 388 387 169 171 182 186 194
347 394 168 180 183 191 193
367 369 384 389 181 189 190 195 118
380 393 178 187 116
368 321 370 395 167 172 174 176 179 117 196 198 199
383 390 396 166 173 175 177 188 114 115 106 105 197 120 124
371 379 381 376 164 163 165 112 108 23 29 31 36 113 107 25 104 30 33 34 35 103 102 119 121 122 123 201 202
372 382 391 162 161 111 152 22 16 26 27 28 32 42 41 38 84 86 101 125 204 203 205 200
320 377 378 160 159 110 153 151 15 11 5 6 43 39 74 82 126 206 207
373 375 109 21 17 10 4 1 44 7 40 89 75 81 80 127 208 210 209
157 158 155 150 13 3 2 8 45 73 77 78 90 91 92 79 100 212 211 225
154 156 18 14 9 20 19 46 72 94 93 98 128 99 96 97
319 374 149 147 148 131 129 130 133 214 213 135 132 224 216
318 317 316 146 61 144 145 48 54 55 49 53 71 136 226 223 218 215 217
303 315 314 143 60 62 50 52 227 220 219
299 301 309 142 59 58 57 51 70 137 228 222 221
302 288 313 310 308 307 141 63 64 68 67 69 66 229
300 287 312 311 305 140 65 138 139
290 304 306 250 252 249 247 230
298 289 286 251 248 246 231
292 291 284 285 260 239 244
296 297 283 253
295 294 293 282 279 261 259 262 255 240 232 245
280 277 278 273 243 241
276 281 268 257 254 238 240
275 272 258 235 242
269 274 263 256 236 237 233
267 270 271 264 234
266 265

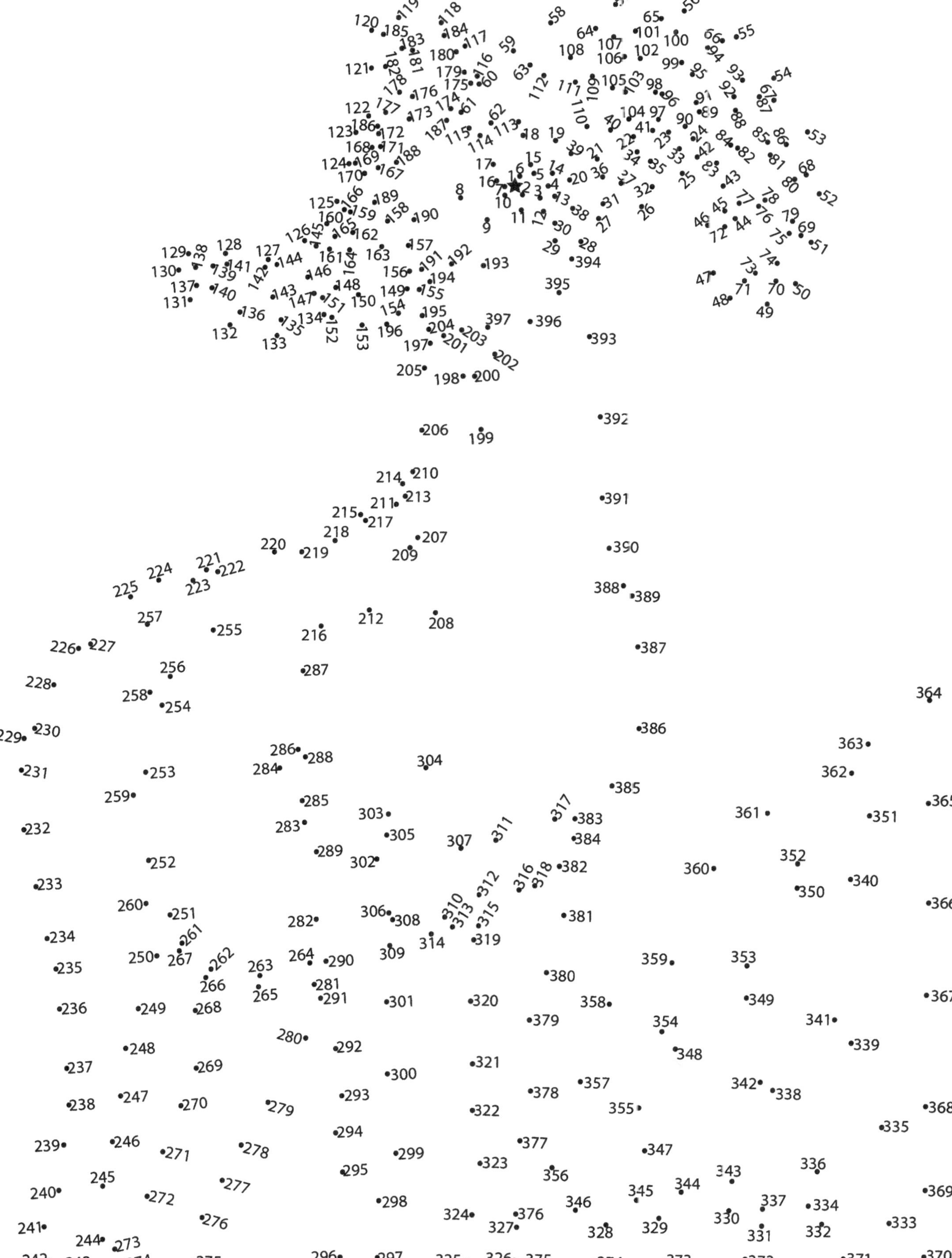

355 356 362 363
354 357 361
352 353 328 327 364
336 332 331 326
350 340 339 335 329 330
338 333 334 358
337 360
349 341 325
347 315 359 321 365
346 351 316 320 322
343 348 342 314
345 309 310 366
308 324
344
303 304 305 311 319 367
299 307 313 317
298 302 300 312 323 368
294 295 306 376 375 318 373 372 369
297 377 374 380 371
293 296 301 269 378 381
291 273 272 270 268 265 379 370 397
290 292 274 266 264 398 388 396
277 276 382 387 391
254 258 263 262 383 395
289 278 271 297 257 259 261 384 386 390 392
275 253 255 256 260 219 389 393
287 288 250 251 226 225 220 385 28 27 26 25 394
286 249 252 227 221 218 214 213 212 16 5 24 75
284 285 280 279 228 217 208 211 29 103 9 23 76
281 246 247 248 232 231 224 222 215 209 30 14 15 20 21 22 74 77
283 245 237 233 230 223 216 207 210 31 16 18 73 78 79
282 244 236 201 204 205 206 33 32 17 64 72 71 80
243 238 200 202 203 235 34 82 81
239 199 198 37 36 63 65 68 70 69 83
242 240 38 35 67
241 196 197 40 39 51 62 66
195 43 42 41 50 61
176 194 44 59 60 84
175 157 177 193 45 53 57 58 85 124 125 126
168 167 182 192 191 49 56 105 115 107 112 121 122
174 181 153 190 46 47 48 54 55 87 95 106 103 104 108 109 111 113 114 116 117 118 119 120 127 128
166 164 178 180 183 143 142 141 86 93 98 100 102 110 129 130 131 132 133 134 135 136 137 138 139 140 144 145 146 147 148 149 150 151 152 154 155 156 158 159 160 161 162 163 169 170 171 172 173 184 185 186 187 188 189 88 89 90 91 92 94 96 97 99 101

44 45 43 46 42 40 47 48 39 41 70 11 49 38 37 7 3 8 2 1 9 36 6 5 4 16 12 51 17 20 18 15 50 34 19 21 13 52 35 33 31 28 24 22 54 32 30 29 27 25 23 14 26 67 410 411 53 56 55 58 68 409 360 359 358 352 57 60 62 66 ★ 408 356 357 353 351 59 64 61 63 65 70 363 361 355 354 350 69 362 347 348 349 300 407 366 364 346 345 340 301 299 406 365 343 344 341 71 395 394 342 339 73 81 72 405 397 396 391 367 336 338 302 74 233 404 403 402 392 393 368 337 335 298 403 388 390 372 371 370 307 80 75 236 238 215 399 389 373 333 334 306 303 297 257 223 172 138 401 398 387 375 332 331 310 304 296 82 235 234 239 181 200 207 193 400 384 386 376 328 313 309 295 258 79 76 240 137 139 192 382 383 378 377 327 312 311 292 259 78 77 241 245 142 171 191 190 279 381 380 379 325 326 316 314 289 294 260 255 83 244 246 141 140 143 189 322 323 324 319 315 293 262 261 254 84 242 136 173 180 182 275 280 318 286 291 267 263 251 85 243 248 135 144 188 321 320 283 290 288 268 266 265 264 252 87 86 247 134 170 145 183 187 278 284 282 271 270 269 102 101 97 90 89 88 250 92 249 133 169 174 179 146 175 186 184 277 276 274 273 103 128 100 96 98 93 147 168 167 176 178 155 104 126 130 99 95 94 132 148 149 164 166 157 156 160 124 123 125 122 107 116 113 109 150 165 163 158 159 161 154 105 106 121 115 117 111 110 120 119 118 114 162 152 151 153
211 219 203 210 212 228 227 204 218 220 229 226 202 209 217 205 197 230 225 213 221 196 231 232 224 216 201 195 237 214 206 208 199 222

211 210 208 206 204 203 201
213 212 207 202 199
214 215 209 205 200 198 197 196
216 137 136 145 194
143 144 146 147 193 73 74
138 134 135 156 155 150 149 72 75
218 132 133 142 157 154 148 192 70 71
217 139 131 151 153 191 68 69 76
219 129 130 158 77
351 140 141 159 14 152 48 49 66 67 79
128 5 8 57 58 50 190 78
353 352 220 13 4 7 6 1 9 15 54 55 56 59 65 80
354 416 222 127 3 2 47 60 51 82
126 160 162 12 11 10 16 46 53 52 61 64 81
221 350 123 17 45 62 63 187 189 83
355 415 223 125 161 163 27 18 19 43 44 3 186 188 84 87
414 348 122 124 164 167 20 21 41 42 185 85 86
349 121 26 22 40 35 91 88
356 413 224 226 119 165 28 25 24 23 31 38 39 37 34 181 89
359 358 412 347 120 168 169 29 30 32 33 180 184 182 92 90
225 344 116 166 170 172 174 177 179 183 93
360 227 118 110 171 173 175 176 178 94 321
357 345 343 109 104 103 99 95 319
383 411 229 338 117 115 113 111 107 105 102 98 96 322
361 228 346 342 339 337 333 114 100 320
362 382 410 230 238 341 112 108 106 327 101 97 318
381 384 329 326 324 316
363 380 409 408 231 336 334 332 330 307 328 309 311 315 317
385 233 237 239 340 335 323 325
364 379 272 274 331 279 282 310 284 314 308
377 365 378 366 232 236 243 245 248 276 306 281 312 313
376 386 234 240 273 285
375 373 369 367 387 235 242 244 246 249 278 280 283
374 372 370 368 388 271 247 275 277 305 304
371 389 407 406 405 270 250 286
390 394 398 403 402 303 287
391 395 399 401 269 302 288
392 393 396 397 400 268 264 260 253 301 297 293 289
267 263 259 256 254 255 298 294 290
266 265 262 258 257 300 299 296 295 292 291

75 37
76 36 38
74 77 35 39
73 80 34 40
64 78 79 81 32 41
65 72 82 25 33 42
63 66 71 83 26 31 30 43
62 67 24 27 29 44
61 84 28 45
68 70 53 52 23 404 403
60 69 85 51 406 412
59 58 54 48 22 46 405
87 86 55 50 47 21 410 41 402
57 56 49 20 407 409
88 17 18 11 10 19 8 414 413 401
89 16 5 4 408 400
90 15 12 13 3 9 399
91 2 8 415
152 151 150 149 92 14 6 7
154 153 230 148 101 100
155 171 146 93 102 106 99 416
156 172 229 145 94 103 98 419 418 417 398
232 231 95 105 97 110 411 412 413
158 170 144 96 104 109 140 114
157 173 143 142 107 108 122 126 415 397
159 175 169 228 233 141 139 128 116 117
174 161 235 127 124 119
160 168 227 234 130 123 118 396
176 162 129 121 120 131
167 133 395
177 163 165 226 236 138 132 385 394 391
164 166 200 249 137 134 384 390 392
178 179 225 245 135 383 386
180 199 201 237 238 248 250 136 382 387 393
224 240 239 244 246 247 274 380 381 389
241 243 251 273 379 388 291
242 252 275 378 377
181 198 202 223 253 272 376 285
182 317 290 292
197 203 222 375 284 289
183 204 221 254 271 276 282 286 299
196 220 374 288 293 297
316 205 255 277
318 195 219 332 270 294 296 300
315 206 218 337 269 373 283
184 194 338 256 268 281 287 295 298
319 324 207 216 217 215 333 343 257 278 371 372 267 265 264 280 361 357 355 301
321 336 339 266 262 279 369 365
314 185 192 193 191 326 208 212 214 334 344 258 259 263 368 364 360 358 354 302
188 190 209 210 211 213 347 349 260 261 366 363 359 356
320 186 187 342 340 346 348 350 351 367 352 353 303
322 325 327 328 329 330 335 345 341
313 312 311 310 309 308 307 306 305 304

386 385 384 389 390 391 392 396 397 398 393 395 394 402 403 404 405 102 383 388 381 382 400 406 407 101 103 104 99 105 106 107 108
374 373 372 379 380 368 369 370 375 376 371 378 366 364 365 363 362 361 360 359 358 357 356 355 354 353 352 351 350 349 348 347 346 345 344 343 342 341 340 339 338 337 336 335 334 333 332 331 330 329 328 327 326 325 324 323 322 321 320 319 318 317 316 315 314 313 312 311 310 309 308 307 306 305 304 303 302 301 300 299 298 297 296 295 294 293 292 291 290 289 288 287 286 285 284 283 282 281 280 279 278 277 276 275 274 273 272 271 270 269 268 267 266 265 264 263 262 261 260 259 258 257 256 255 254 253 252 251 250 249 248 247 246 245 244 243 242 241 240 239 238 237 236 235 234 233 232 231 230 229 228 227 226 225 224 223 222 221 220 219 218 217 216 215 214 213 212 211 210 209 208 207 206 205 204 203 202 201 200 199 198 197 196 195 194 193 192 191 190 189 188 187 186 185 184 183 182 181 180 179 178 177 176 175 174 173 172 171 170 169 168 167 166 165 164 163 162 161 160 159 158 157 156 155 154 153 152 151 150 149 148 147 146 145 144 143 142 141 140 139 138 137 136 135 134 133 132 131 130 129 128 127 126 125 124 123 122 121 120 119 118 117 116 115 114 113 112 111 110 109
1 2 3 4 5 6 7 8 9 10 11 12 13 14 15 16 17 18 19 20 21 22 23 24 25 26 27 28 29 30 31 32 33 34 35 36 37 38 39 40 41 42 43 44 45 46 47 48 49 50 51 52 53 54 55 56 57 58 59 60 61 62 63 64 65 66 67 68 69 70 71 72 73 74 75 76 77 78 79 80 81 82 83 84 85 86 87 88 89 90 91 92 93 94 95 96 97 98 100
408 409 410 411 412 413 414 415 416 417 418 419 420 421 422 377 367

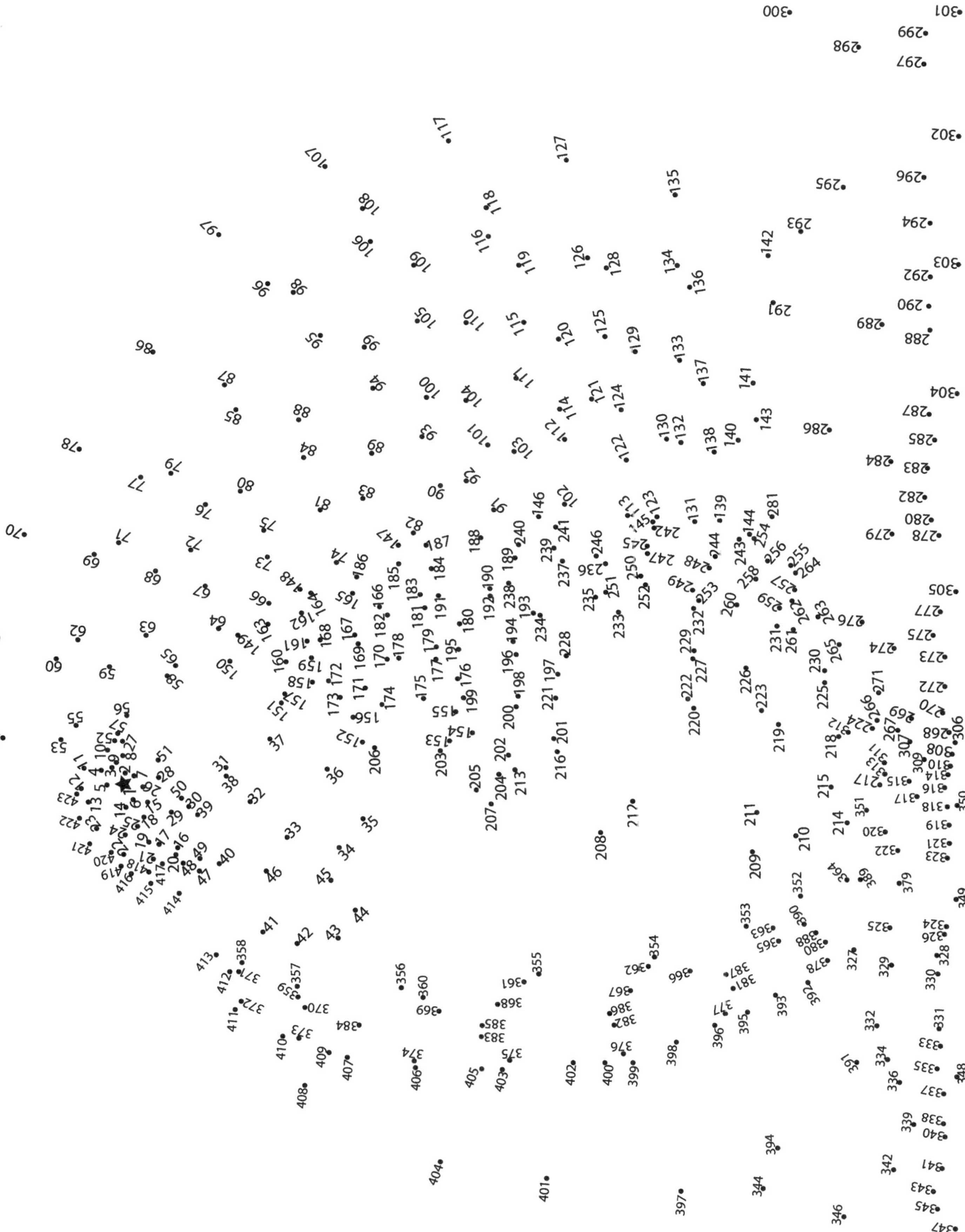

1 2 3 4 5 6 7 8 9 10 11 12 13 14 15 16 17 18 19 20 21 22 23 24 25 26 27 28 29 30 31 32 33 34 35 36 37 38 39 40 41 42 43 44 45 46 47 48 49 50 51 52 53 54 55 56 57 58 59 60 61 62 63 64 65 66 67 68 69 70 71 72 73 74 75 76 77 78 79 80 81 82 83 84 85 86 87 88 89 90 91 92 93 94 95 96 97 98 99 100 101 102 103 104 105 106 107 108 109 110 111 112 113 114 115 116 117 118 119 120 121 122 123 124 125 126 127 128 129 130 131 132 133 134 135 136 137 138 139 140 141 142 143 144 145 146 147 148 149 150 151 152 153 154 155 156 157 158 159 160 161 162 163 164 165 166 167 168 169 170 171 172 173 174 175 176 177 178 179 180 181 182 183 184 185 186 187 188 189 190 191 192 193 194 195 196 197 198 199 200 201 202 203 204 205 206 207 208 209 210 211 212 213 214 215 216 217 218 219 220 221 222 223 224 225 226 227 228 229 230 231 232 233 234 235 236 237 238 239 240 241 242 243 244 245 246 247 248 249 250 251 252 253 254 255 256 257 258 259 260 261 262 263 264 265 266 267 268 269 270 271 272 273 274 275 276 277 278 279 280 281 282 283 284 285 286 287 288 289 290 291 292 293 294 295 296 297 298 299 300 301 302 303 304 305 306 307 308 309 310 311 312 313 314 315 316 317 318 319 320 321 322 323 324 325 326 327 328 329 330 331 332 333 334 335 336 337 338 339 340 341 342 343 344 345 346 347 348 349 350 351 352 353 354 355 356 357 358 359 360 361 362 363 364 365 366 367 368 369 370 371 372 373 374 375 376 377 378 379 380 381 382 383 384 385 386 387 388 389 390 391 392 393 394 395 396 397 398 399 400 401 402 403 404 405 406 407 408 409 410 411 412 413 414 415 416 417 418 419 420 421 422 423 424

415 417 414
16 15 14 13 12 416 418 413
17 20 7 4 6 11 421 422
27 18 19 3 1 5 420 419 412
21 25 26 8 2 10 423 411
23 24 9
28 29 31 32 33 424 410
30 34 35 409
37 36 44 425 427 408
38 43 428 429 407
39 45 426 406
42 41 405 404
40 46 430
47 431 433
48 432 434
49 435 102
50 436 437 99
51 254 54 55 58 100 101 148
52 53 56 57 59 60 98 97 103 142
249 250 251 252 253 255 61 62 63 64 96 95 104 137 136 149 153 159 195 203 202 200
248 264 263 262 261 260 259 258 257 256 271 272 94 105 138 139 135 140 152 160 196 204 380
247 265 266 267 268 269 270 273 274 275 93 92 134 150 151 161 166 194 197 199 379 375
246 280 279 278 277 276 65 106 133 164 153 193 198 205 374 376
245 298 297 296 295 283 284 285 286 91 132 168 192 206 373 378 377
299 282 66 90 107 131 169 191 207 366 372
244 300 301 302 303 304 292 291 287 288 72 71 108 114 130 170 175 208 367 371 365
315 314 313 312 311 310 305 290 289 67 68 70 89 115 113 129 171 174 190 368 370 364
243 316 306 308 73 69 109 112 128 176 172 173 189 210 369 363
317 74 110 111 188 211
242 318 319 320 321 322 323 324 307 75 87 127 179 178 187 212 362
330 329 328 327 326 325 76 117 180 186 213 361
241 331 332 333 334 335 336 337 77 118 123 126 181 185 214 360
343 342 341 340 339 338 80 86 124 125 182 122 215 216 359
240 344 345 346 347 348 349 81 78 79 183 184 217 218 358
82 85 119 121 219 220 221
83 84 120 350 351 352 353 354 355 356 357 222
239 238 237 236 235 234 233 232 231 230 229 228 227 226 225 224 223

398 397 396
399 395
394
400 390 391 393 389 392
401 145 388
402 387
403 386
144 146 385 156
143 147 384 155 157 383
141 158 201 382 154 381
137 136 149 159 195

333• •334 •335 332• 331• •336 •337 330• •338 329• 328• 327• 324• 341 •340 326• 325 308 307 306 342 343 •344 •305 345 302 301 •290 346 289 •300 •288 287 •347 •348

335 339 338 337 340 339 444 323 322 312 311 310 388 389 385 382 381 379 380 391 390 384 383 295 294 293 296 297 298 304 303 292 291 286 285 •349 350 351 352

397 395 396 394 393 392 408 371 370 372 376 377 375 373 282 369 374 283 284 281 280 368 354 353 355 356 357 358 359 360 361 362 363 364 365 366 367 279 278 277 276 275 274 273 272 271 270 269 268 267 266 265 264 263 262 261 260 259 258 257 256 255 254 253 252 251 250 249 248 247 246 245 244 243 242 241 240 239 238 237 236 235 234 233 232 231 230 229 228 227 226 225 224 223 222 221 220 219 218 217 216 215 214 213 212 211 210 209 208 207 206 205 204 203 202 201 200 199 198 197 196 195 194 193 192 191 190 189 188 187 186 185 184 183 182 181 180 179 178 177 176 175 174 173 172 171 170 169 168 167 166 165 164 163 162 161 160 159 158 157 156 155 154 153 152 151 150 149 148 147 146 145 144 143 142 141 140 139 138 137 136 135 134 133 132 131 130 129 128 127 126 125 124 123 122 121 120 119 118 117 116 115 114 113 112 111 110 109 108 107 106 105 104 103 102 101 100 99 98 97 96 95 94 93 92 91 90 89 88 87 86 85 84 83 82 81 80 79 78 77 76 75 74 73 72 71 70 69 68 67 66 65 64 63 62 61 60 59 58 57 56 55 54 53 52 51 50 49 48 47 46 45 44 43 42 41 40 39 38 37 36 35 34 33 32 31 30 29 28 27 26 25 24 23 22 21 20 19 18 17 16 15 14 13 12 11 10 9 8 7 6 5 4 3 2 1

400 401 402 403 404 405 406 407 408 409 410 411 412 413 414 415 416 417 418 419 420 421 422 423 424 425 426 427 428 429 430 431 432 433 434 435 436 437 438 439 440 441 442 443 444

189 489 194 450 449 448 436 435 434
490 192 193
191 188 196 176 175 172 171
497 199 200 173
187 198 184 178 177 174 154 155 160 162 163 170 451
185 183 201 153 202 159 156 217 161 165 164 169 452 453 437 447 433
186 182 152 179 181 203 166 218 438
180 151 457 216 215 219 168 439 446 432
150 205 204 158 214 220 167 445
138 139 149 148 206 221 223 222 110 381 443 444 423 431 430
140 141 147 137 146 207 213 224 441 442
136 135 143 144 145 208 209 212 380 382 422 424 428
128 131 127 132 123 133 120 122 121 114 113 233 234 210 211 235 236 379 383 425 427 429
33 34 35 119 118 124 134 112 110 111 232 228 227 237 377 384 426
40 36 37 129 130 116 109 102 101 231 230 226 376 378 420 419 418 417
32 39 31 41 38 42 43 126 125 117 107 106 108 104 105 103 229 225 375 373 372 392 385 386 387 416 415 414 413
29 27 26 25 44 46 47 48 49 85 94 99 98 374 371 391 390 389 388
9 8 3 7 2 6 1 17 28 19 24 20 22 45 23 50 51 82 83 84 86 87 92 100 239 238 370 341 340 393 394 395 396 397 410 411 412
10 4 11 5 12 16 15 14 53 54 52 73 74 81 80 79 88 90 91 240 242 243 244 245 241 246 247 248 249 250 251 267 268 342 354 346 345 337 347 348 331 333 335 336 398 399 400 401 402 403 404 405 406 407 408 409
57 58 63 56 64 65 72 75 76 77 78 252 253 254 255 256 257 258 259 260 261 262 263 264 265 266 269 270 271 272 273 274 275 276 277 278 279 280 281 282 283 285 287 288 289 290 291 292 293 294 295 296 297 298 299 300 301 302 303 304 305 306 307 308 309 310 311 312 313 314 315 316 317 318 319 320 321 322 323 324 325 326 327 328 329 330 332 334 338 339 343 344 349 350 351 352 353 355 356 357 358 359 360 361 362 363 364 365 366 367 368 369 59 60 61 62 66 67 68 69 70 71

436 435 434 431 430
437 440 439 422 432 429 427
441 442 443 438 424 428 426
444 419 420 165 423 47 45
451 450 447 446 445 418 167 49 48 46 43
452 448 449 416 417 421 163 425 51 50 16 44
415 414 413 169 168 166 162 161 52 18 47 15 42
453 455 454 412 171 170 172 156 158 160 53 19 7 2 6 41
456 411 409 408 174 155 159 54 20 21 8 3 5 13 39 40
457 459 460 401 173 176 154 95 94 92 91 90 55 56 22 9 4 1 11 30 38
458 462 461 410 406 407 402 400 175 153 96 98 159 88 57 58 60 23 10 29 12 36 37
463 464 466 465 403 397 396 177 178 152 97 151 100 102 89 86 59 24 25 31 35 34
467 469 405 399 395 391 179 180 150 149 99 101 104 87 83 61 62 28 33 69
468 470 398 394 390 388 181 182 183 148 147 145 103 105 106 85 82 80 63 26 27 32 70
471 404 475 393 389 387 374 372 371 185 186 146 143 108 84 81 79 64 66 68 64
472 474 381 385 386 383 375 370 369 367 187 188 189 190 144 141 107 110 112 77 65 67 72 71
473 380 382 384 379 378 376 368 366 191 192 194 142 139 109 111 114 78 116 76 75 73 120
353 351 350 354 355 356 357 365 364 363 193 195 140 137 135 113 115 117 74 121 119
352 349 347 345 346 377 361 360 200 198 138 136 133 127 125 122 118
348 344 342 341 358 362 359 201 202 204 209 131 129 126 124 123
343 339 340 330 329 324 320 206 205 208 210 134 132 130 215 128 218 219 220
337 333 331 328 325 323 321 319 236 237 207 235 211 212 213 214 216 217 221
338 332 327 326 322 318 287 286 285 284 238 234 233 231 230 227 228 226 225 224 223 222
316 317 289 288 282 240 239 229 247 248
315 314 313 290 291 283 281 241 242 244 243 226 249 250
312 311 310 309 292 293 294 280 279 245 246
308 307 306 305 304 295 296 278 277 254 276 253 251
303 302 301 300 299 298 297 275
255 274 272 271 270
256 273 269 268 267
257 262 263 264 265 266
258 261
259 260

46 47 48 52 51 49 53

42 43 50 61 54 41 44 45 62 60 40 66 55 63 67 59 56 39 18 17 68 65 57

19 4 5 16 38 20 10 9 1 32 6 69 64 72 58 103 37 21 12 8 7 15 70 71 73 102 101 310

24 36 11 13 14 94 95 99 100 104 133 134 132 135 114 113

23 84 85 89 93 98 315 311 131 129 130 112 115 137 139 140 128 127

25 30 35 79 83 80 86 97 96 314 312 316 106 105 126 121 120 116 165 164 141 135 138

26 31 29 34 78 82 81 88 92 91 90 74 313 317 309 107 125 124 123 111 117 118 166 171 170 169 163 142

28 77 87 76 75 394 318 319 109 108 122 199 202 197 190 196 172 173 167 168 161 162 160 143

27 32 33 391 395 393 321 320 322 308 110 203 200 201 194 193 175 180 159 144 145

398 396 389 390 388 323 324 226 225 204 209 210 191 195 179 178 176 177 183 158 148 146

399 391 392 387 327 307 325 326 228 227 224 205 208 189 211 188 192 187 186 185 182 181 153 147 149 150

400 485 484 483 328 329 330 223 219 206 207 212 157 184 156 155 152 154 151

401 477 481 482 478 385 306 222 217 221 386

476 475 479 383 384 331 231 230 216 220 218 213

402 480 382 332 333 232 214 474 334 305 215

403 471 473 381 380 234 233 451 472 470 469 379 235 236

404 405 468 377 335 336 304 406 407 378 337

408 450 466 465 467 376 338 303 237 409 410 449 452 464 375 374 239 238

411 445 442 463 372 373 341 302 340 240 443 372 301 242 241 244 243 300 245

412 413 448 444 461 462 342 343 344 414 438 439 453 460 440 459 371 361

415 436 434 435 458 370 362 360 345 346 348 299 246 347 349

447 437 433 456 457 368 367 369 363 366 359 357 358 350 247 293 298 297 288 290 296

416 428 429 430 432 421 422 420 455 424 423 419 365 364 356 355 352 351 353 354 249 250 251 291 292 287 286 258 259 253 252

274 273 268 269 272 275 270 276 271 267 263 278 277 282 262 266 264 295 279 283 281 294 284 280 261 265 255 289 285 256 254 260 257 286 290

40 39 38 37
43 16
41 42 13 6 5 12 17 36 35 34 33 32 31
80 79 77 44 15 14 1 7 2 3 4 11 18 30 26 25
84 83 76 45 46 6 8 19 28 27
81 49 48 10 29 20 24
85 75 50 47 9 22 21 23
87 82 78 74 51 488 487
88 86 73 52
89 90 72 70 69
91 71 68 66 53 67 486
95 92 93 64 54 56 58
96 97 98 94 63 65 55 129 484 485
100 103 99 62 57 59
101 102 105 104 60
106 107 108 118 61 128 130 483
109 110 116 119 127 481 482
112 111 117 115 126 131 480
113 114 120 122 121 123 124 125 132 478 479
155 154 153 133 135 477
156 158 152 134 136 475 476
280 157 150 137
279 299 159 151 161 149 138 474
301 281 160 178 147 140 472 473
278 282 179 162 139 469
300 298 304 302 283 177 164 148 41 468 470
277 295 180 182 163 146 467 471 465 466
307 303 296 181 176 165 144 142 220 464
305 294 284 183 174 145 143 221
293 291 285 175 166 167 218 463
306 292 286 184 185 173 168 219 170 222 461 462
276 308 290 287 172 169 217 223 460
309 288 314 186 210 211 213 171 215 224
275 289 313 337 334 315 188 203 202 209 212 214 225 254 455 457 459 447
310 312 331 187 190 189 198 200 208 207 216 453 456 458 448 446
274 338 332 330 329 316 191 194 196 201 204 205 206 227 452 451 443 445
311 335 333 328 252 192 199 197 226 229 450
340 339 336 324 325 326 327 347 346 195 228 231 233 449 444
273 321 322 323 318 348 193 253 251 230 235 442 440
341 320 319 345 254 250 249 248 232 234 236 441 439
351 350 349 360 247 237 438 436
272 342 384 246 245 244 239 240 435 434 433
352 362 343 344 359 255 261 243 242 241 238 437
373 363 361 256 257 258 259 260 412 413 418 417 411 419 414 421 423 424 415 416 240 432 431
271 372 369 364 366 365 358 389 385 393 262 405 404 402 403 406 410 420 422 409 408 427 429 430 428 425
374 368 353 371 367 357 386 390 394 398 263 411
270 354 375 377 355 356 370 380 383 388 395 396 399 264 401 407
376 378 268 379 381 382 387 266 391 265 400
269

58 70 71 57 69 72 59 67 68 56 65 66 73 60 62 64 74 79 55 61 63 75 77 78 54 76 53 52

87 88 101 89 90 102 86 92 100 85 91 93 95 103 94 97 99 80 84 83 96 98 104 81 82 105

41 47 40 12 5 1 106 42 48 46 39 13 6 4 51 49 50 38 7 23 10 107 50 43 44 45 14 8 9 108 500 120 18 17 16 142 144 145 146 147 119 37 19 26 27 60 143 499 20 25 28 15 41 148 121 118 36 21 24 23 32 140 498 497 122 35 22 33 137 10 39 496 495 117 116 115 113 112 135 136 493 123 125 114 133 204 494 474 124 127 129 134 203 473 492 490 488 128 132 486 205 428 472 475 476 126 130 131 487 471 470 491 489 484 201 435 469 467 468 478 480 482 485 202 466 477 479 481 330 465 464 391 392 329 331 200 427 463 390 328 332 206 199 429 425 421 393 389 327 333 198 208 447 436 423 395 394 326 325 334 207 197 96 190 189 158 157 159 434 462 388 322 324 336 213 212 238 186 160 161 162 441 437 430 396 357 350 387 337 215 237 239 244 184 163 272 276 286 294 446 433 422 461 352 320 216 217 236 242 249 183 164 271 274 282 291 298 440 431 426 460 354 319 386 338 218 240 245 250 165 166 270 268 293 448 442 438 418 420 398 459 356 318 219 235 246 248 182 167 275 285 299 445 432 399 361 351 385 339 317 220 251 168 284 300 443 439 417 419 458 400 347 348 221 234 232 255 181 269 267 265 415 457 401 363 346 384 340 374 315 252 257 254 169 180 170 301 444 412 414 416 402 360 344 383 371 373 314 222 233 231 229 258 260 179 171 266 264 450 455 409 404 403 365 362 379 341 342 370 372 313 308 224 223 253 175 178 176 172 302 413 454 408 405 364 343 382 381 380 378 377 376 312 309 310 225 226 227 259 261 262 263 411 453 410 407 406 366 367 368 369 311 307 306 305 304 303

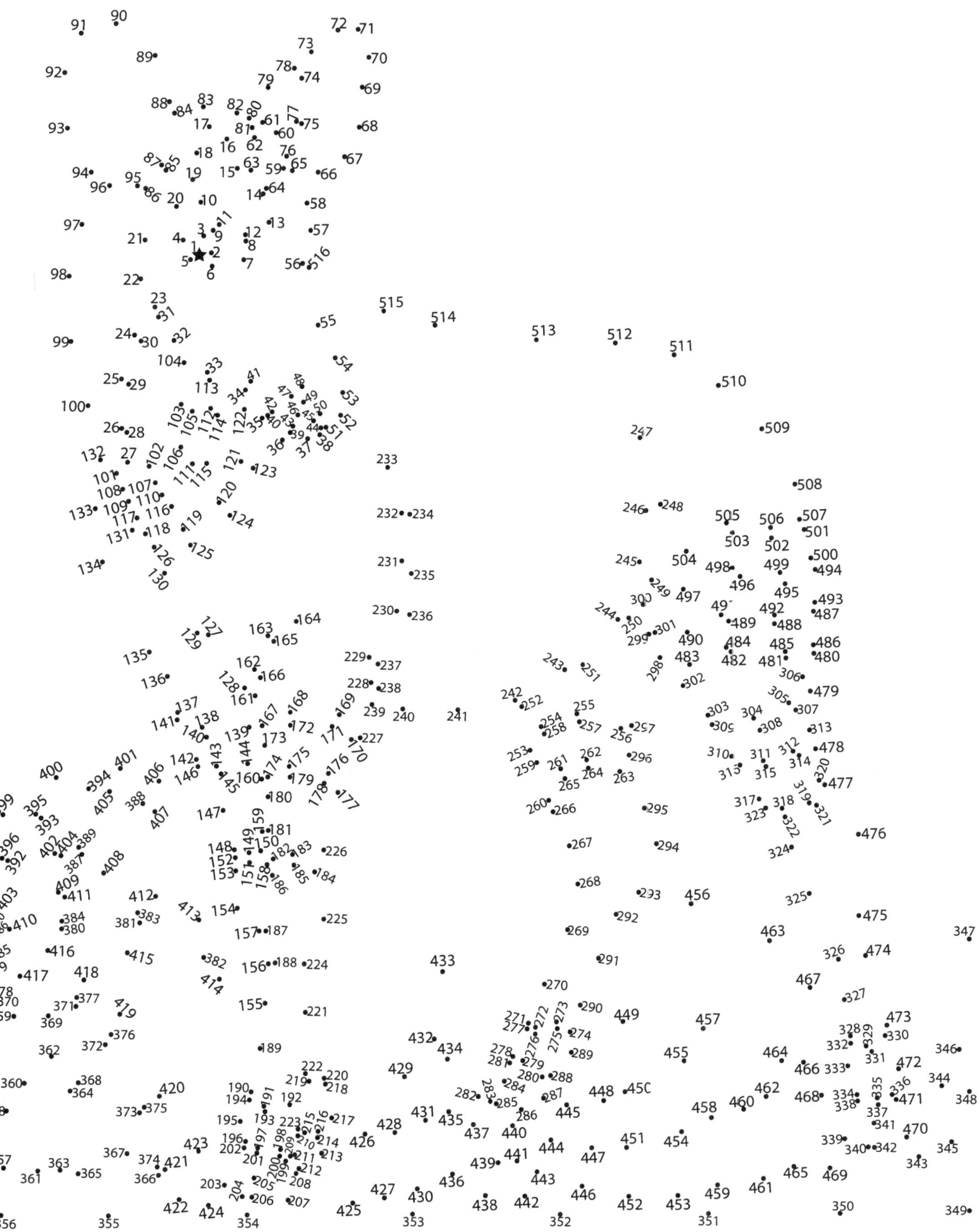

*Enjoy a couple of bonus
images from our other
Dot-to-Dot Books*

Find our books on Amazon.

Easy to Read Dot-to-Dots
Large Print Puzzles from 303-563 Dots

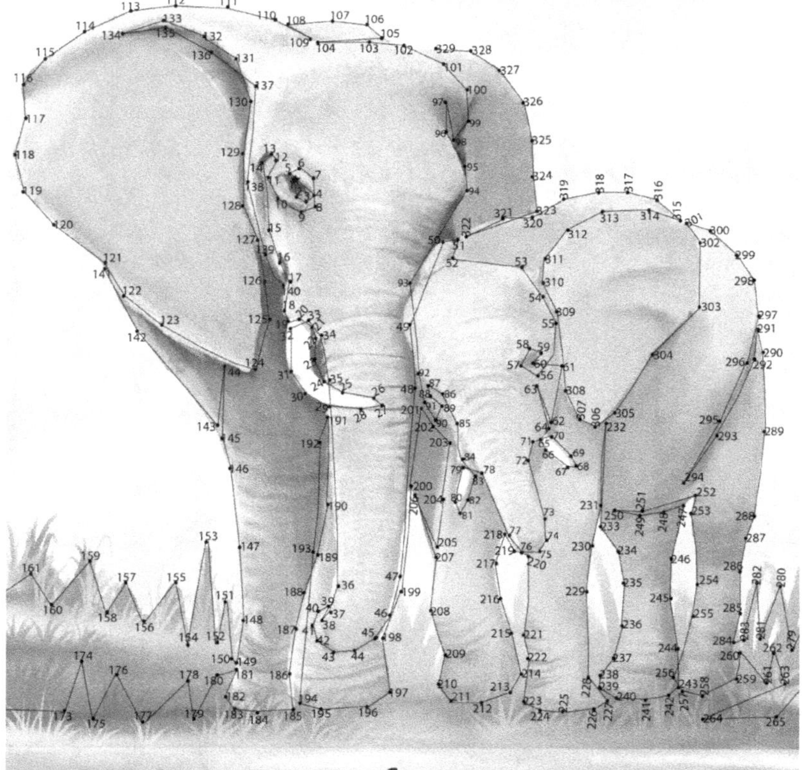

241
236 240 242 278 276 279 280 281 282 283 285
237 213 239 238 209 208 274 277
238 243 245 207 246 206 281 270
235 214 212 244 210 244 277 266 264 284 286
229 230 231 217 234 215 198 199 200 211 247 205 273 252 275 268 287
228 227 219 218 216 197 196 201 249 204 250 251 271 263 262
185 225 226 224 223 220 195 202 203 248 123 254 253 255 260 288 289
184 186 178 187 188 179 222 221 191 180 192 194 181 182 154 153 152 122 124 257 256 258 269 290 291
183 176 175 174 172 167 163 156 117 157 110 150 121 145 155 165 193 151 125 144 131 126 130 134 135 143 142 141 259 261
177 168 171 162 107 108 159 109 118 116 147 111 115 119 114 127 129 133 136 138 139 140 2 8 292
161 169 170 160 106 105 104 103 102 100 101 90 85 112 113 128 86 89 88 87 45 24 23 14 13 12 16 11 17 10 9 137 4 7 293
95 96 97 98 99 83 84 91 82 75 81 80 76 79 78 77 56 25 22 21 26 32 3 34 5 294
94 93 92 74 65 54 58 55 57 44 46 27 38 28 29 30 31 35 36 299 297
72 73 68 53 43 47 39 37 42 40 41 48 301 302 300 298 295 296
71 70 62 63 60 61 59 52 51 50 49 303 1

Landmarks Dot-to-Dot for Adults
Puzzles from 171 to 889 Dots

•4

5• •3
2• •6

9•
•8
1★10
•16
14• 18
15 17
13 24• 19•
12• •25 31 23 •20
29 33• •22
30 32
11• 28• 40 34 •21
41 51 •35
27• 42 49 53 •39
43• 47 38• •36
48 50 52 55
26• 65 64 63 54
46• 75 78 62• 56 •37
45• 66 81 •57
•72 61
73 74 76 77 79 •80 82 84 •58
94 93 114 92 91 83 •60
44• 67 71 111 117 85 •59
68• 70 •95 90 •86
108 110 112 113 115 116 118 120 •89
109• 135 134 133 119 •87
107 149 152 132 121 88
136 •146 155 131 •123
106• 148 150 151 153 154 122 •124
137 147 224 223 222 221• 56 158• •130
143 145 144 157 •125
•105 225 129
69• 142 181• •182 220• 159 160 163 •164
96• 138 180• •183 219• •126
97• 101 104
100 141 226

139
230 229 140
234• 98 102 231 228 •227
235• 99 103 247
236• 245 232 246 175 176
233
174 •177 186• •189 169

248
249 213• 170• 171
237 212
238• 250 •251 210• •211
239• 240 253• •252 209• •208
254• •255 206• •207
257• •256 205• •204
258• •259 202• •203
261• •260 201• •200
241• 262 •263 198• •199
242• 265• •264 197• •196
266• •267 194• •195
269• •268 193• •192
243• 244 270 271• 173 178 179 184 185 190• •191
172

128• •127
161• 162• •216
218• 217• •215
187 188 214 165 166 167 •168

Answer Key

(start from top left to right)

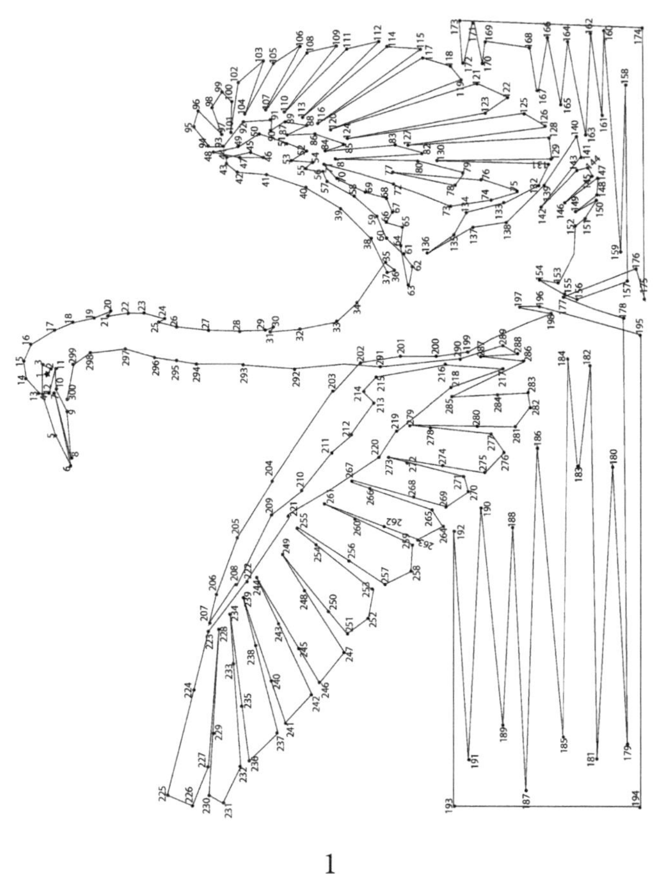

1

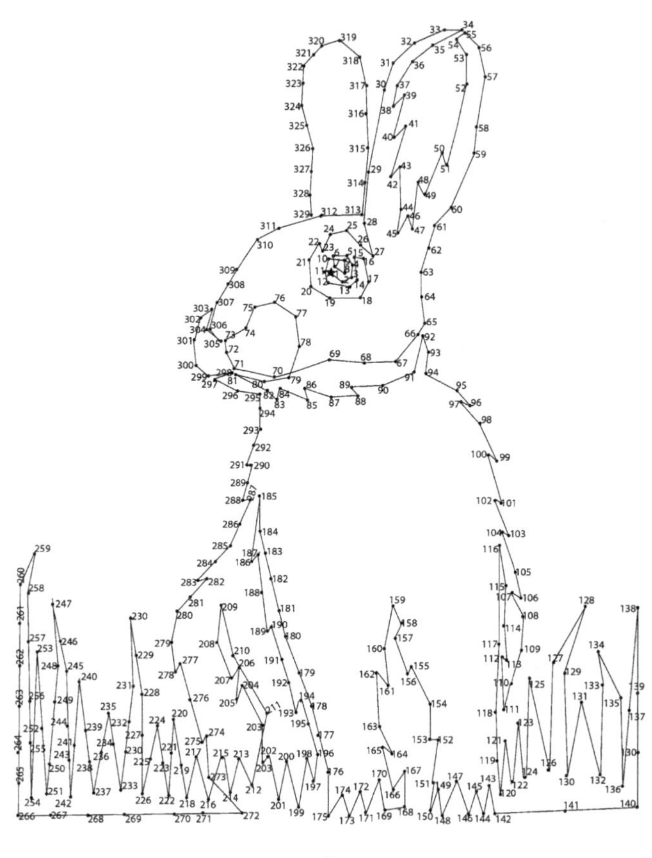

2

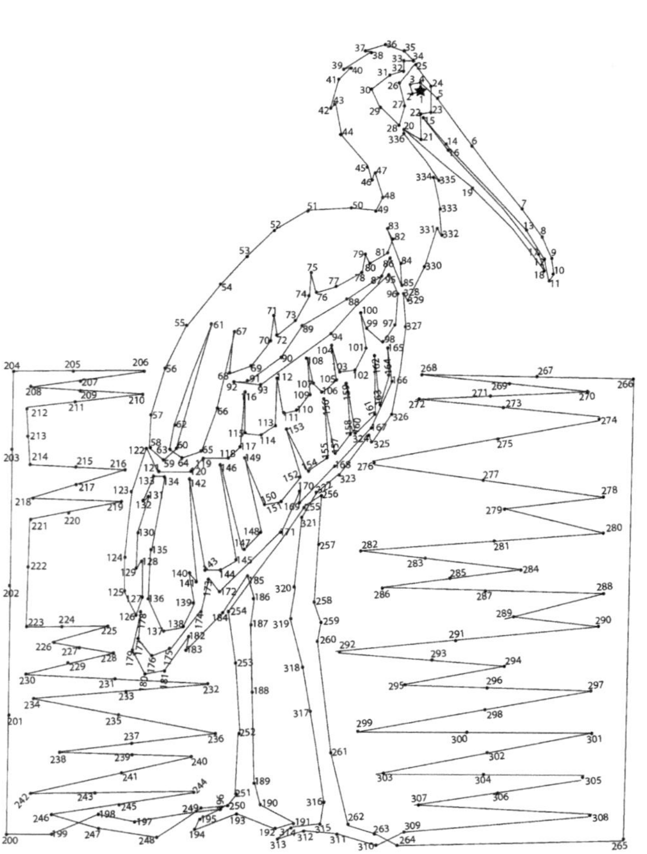

3

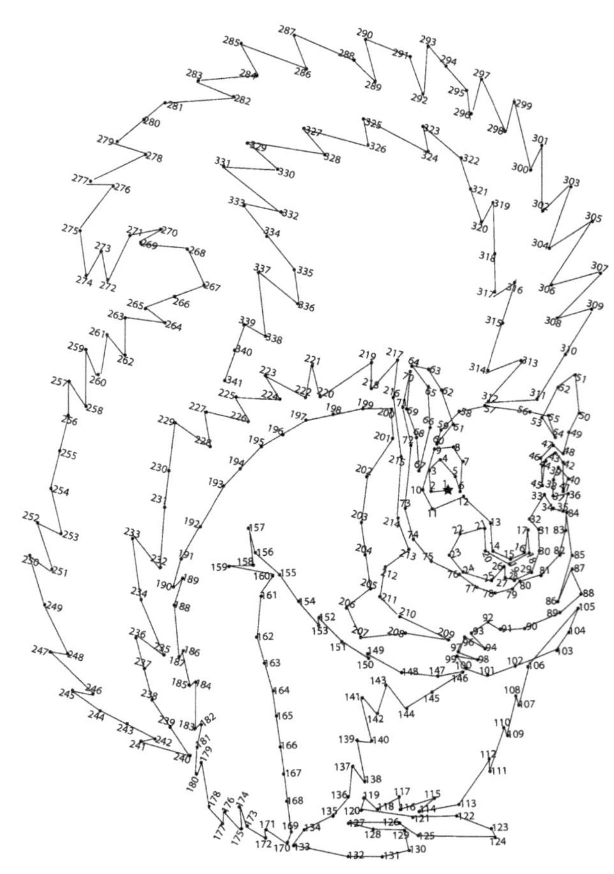

4

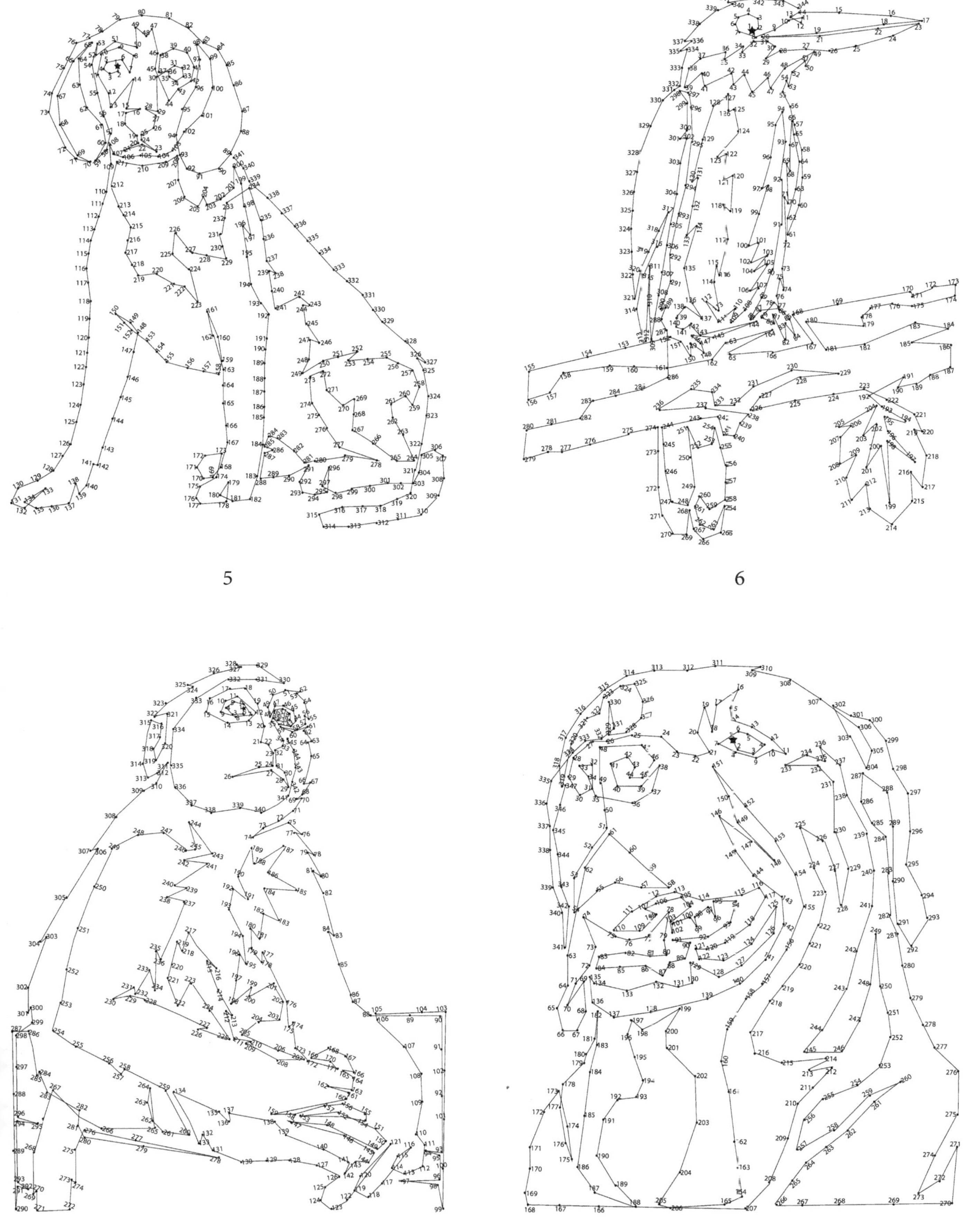

5

6

7

8

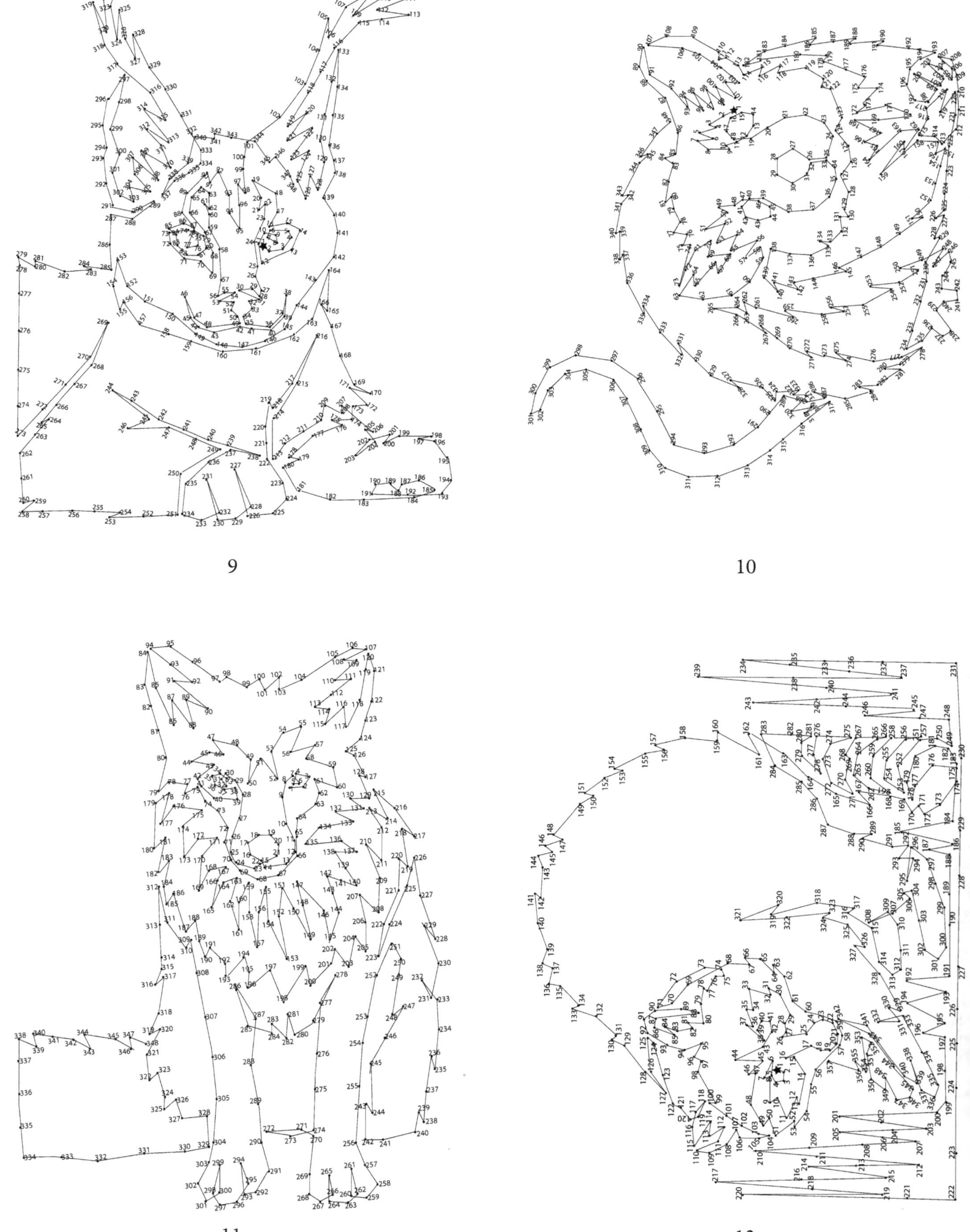

9

10

11

12

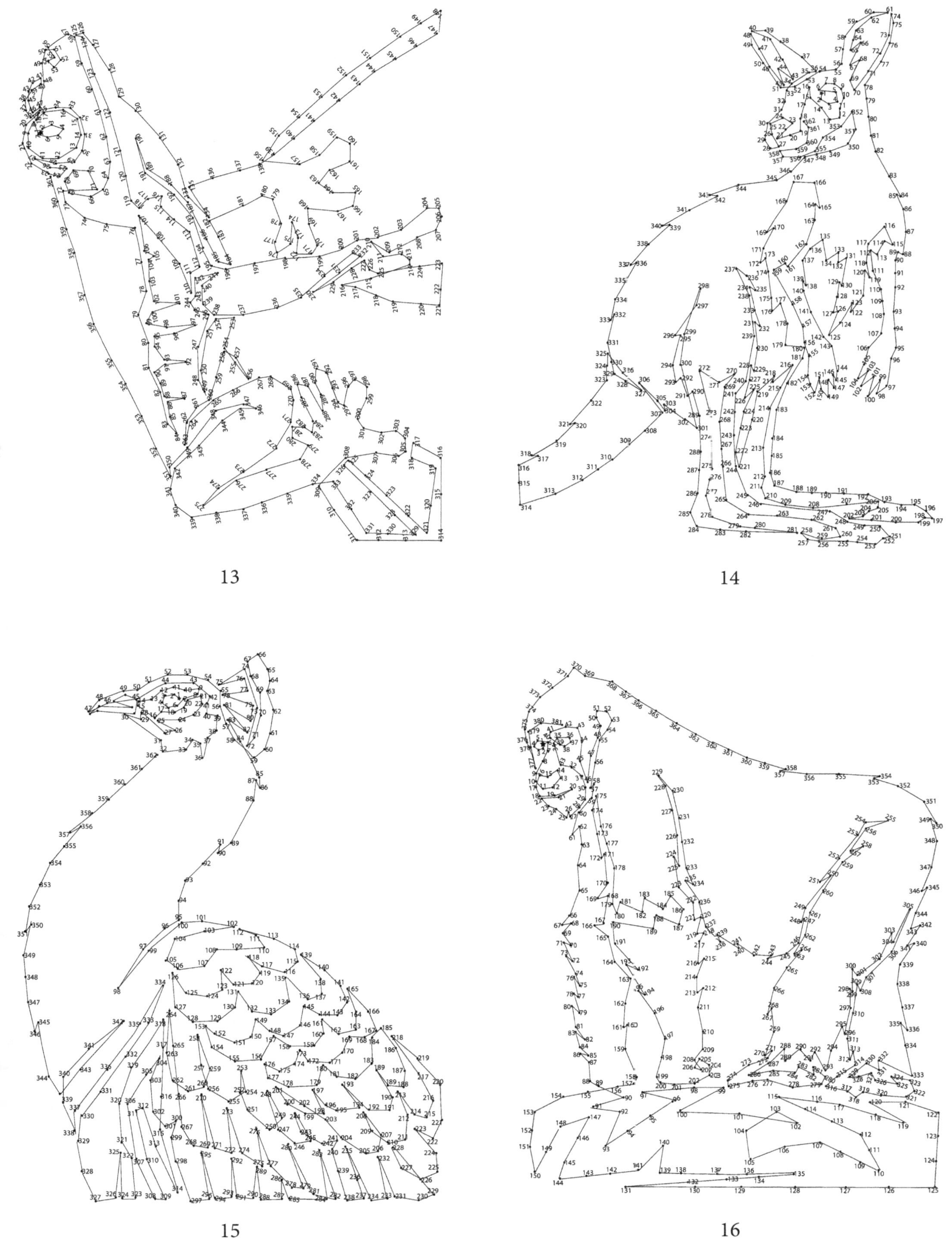

13

14

15

16

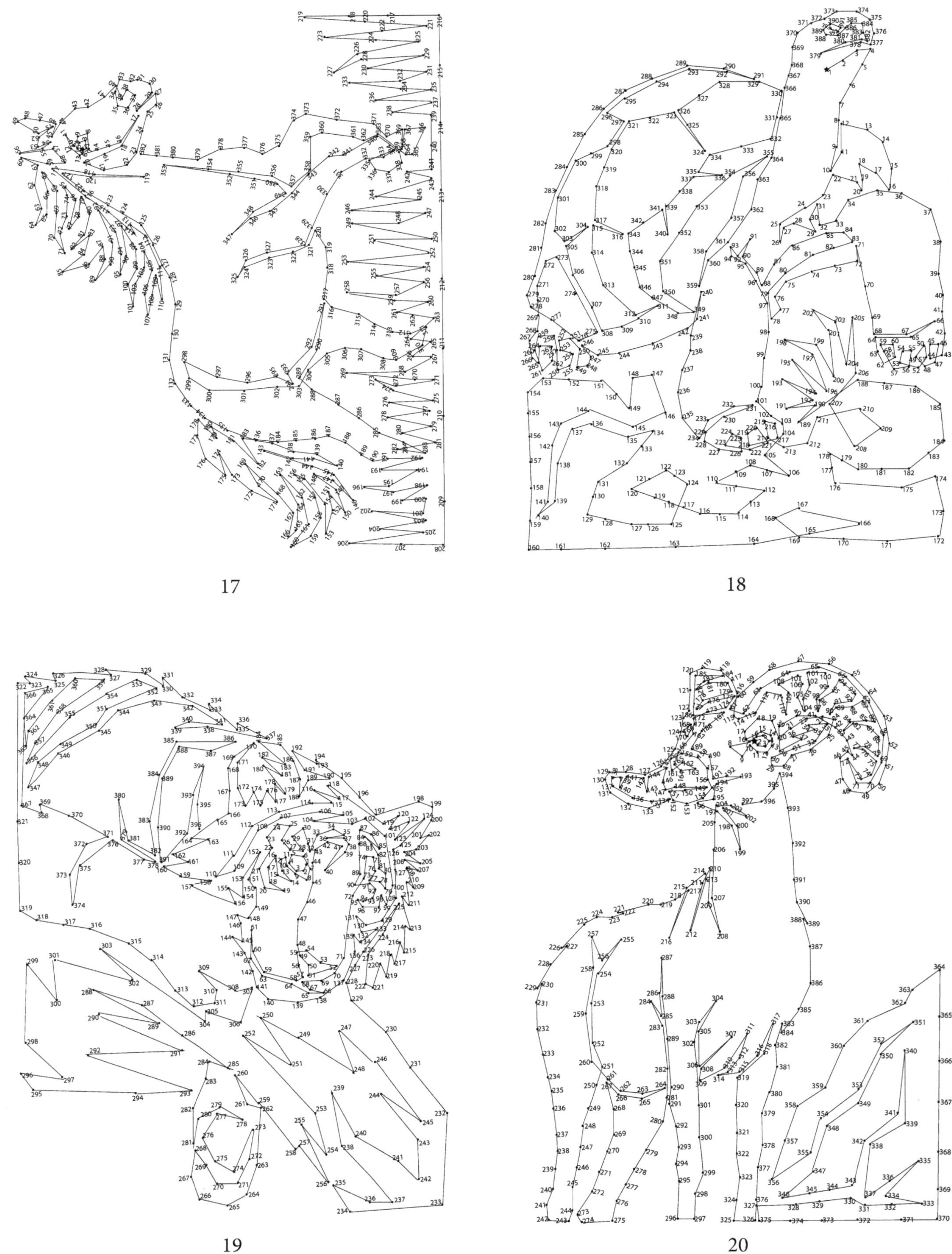

17

18

19

20

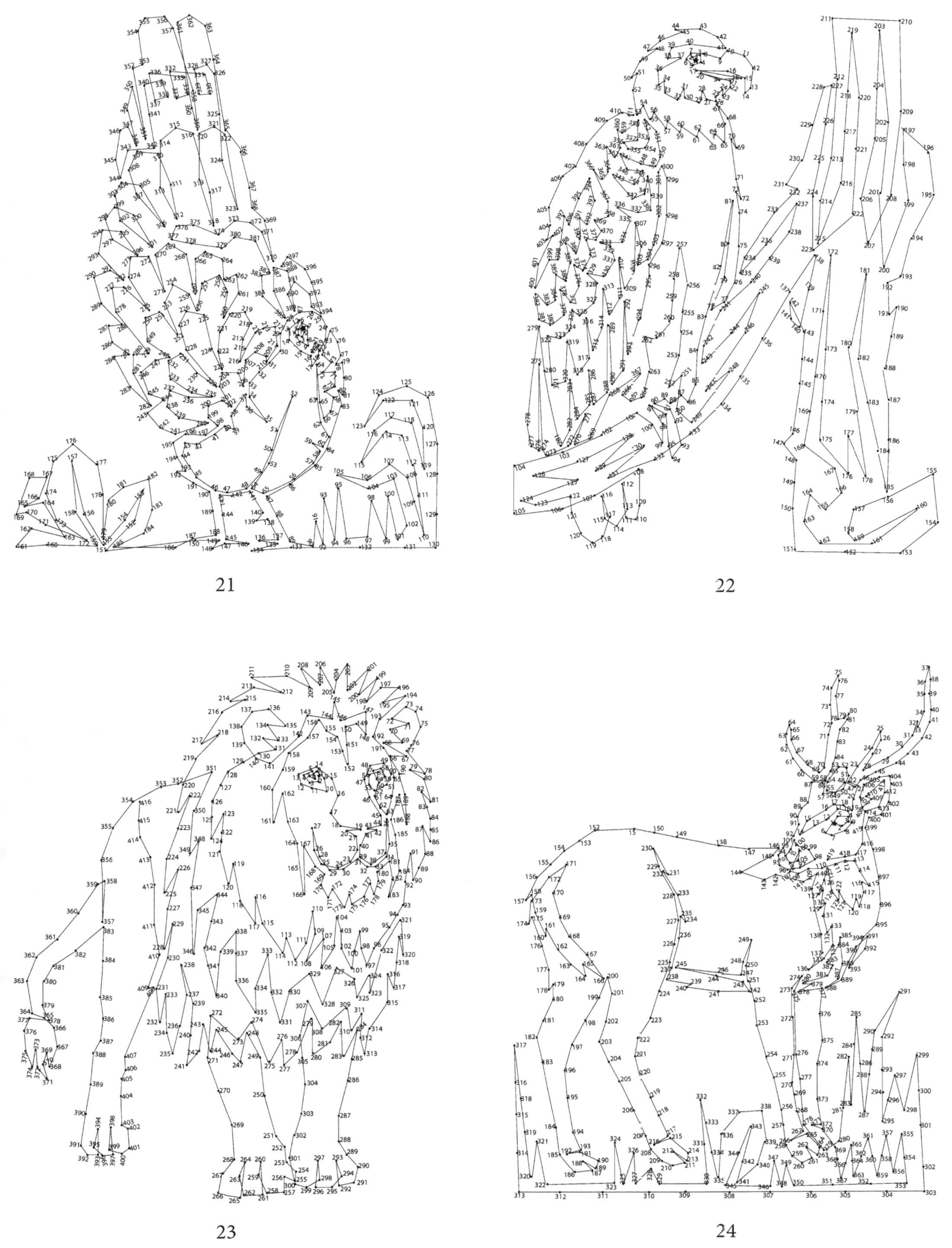

21

22

23

24

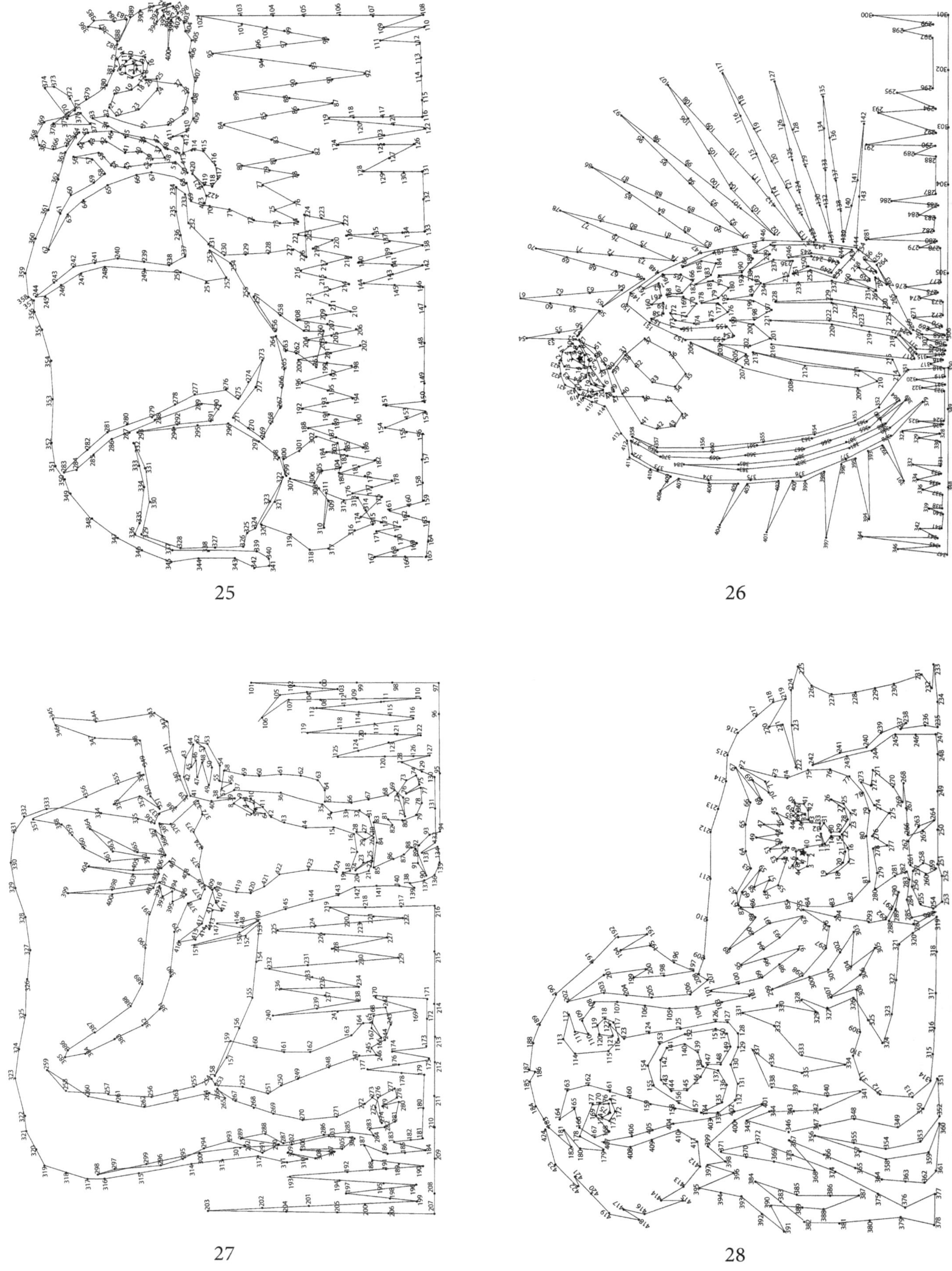

25

26

27

28

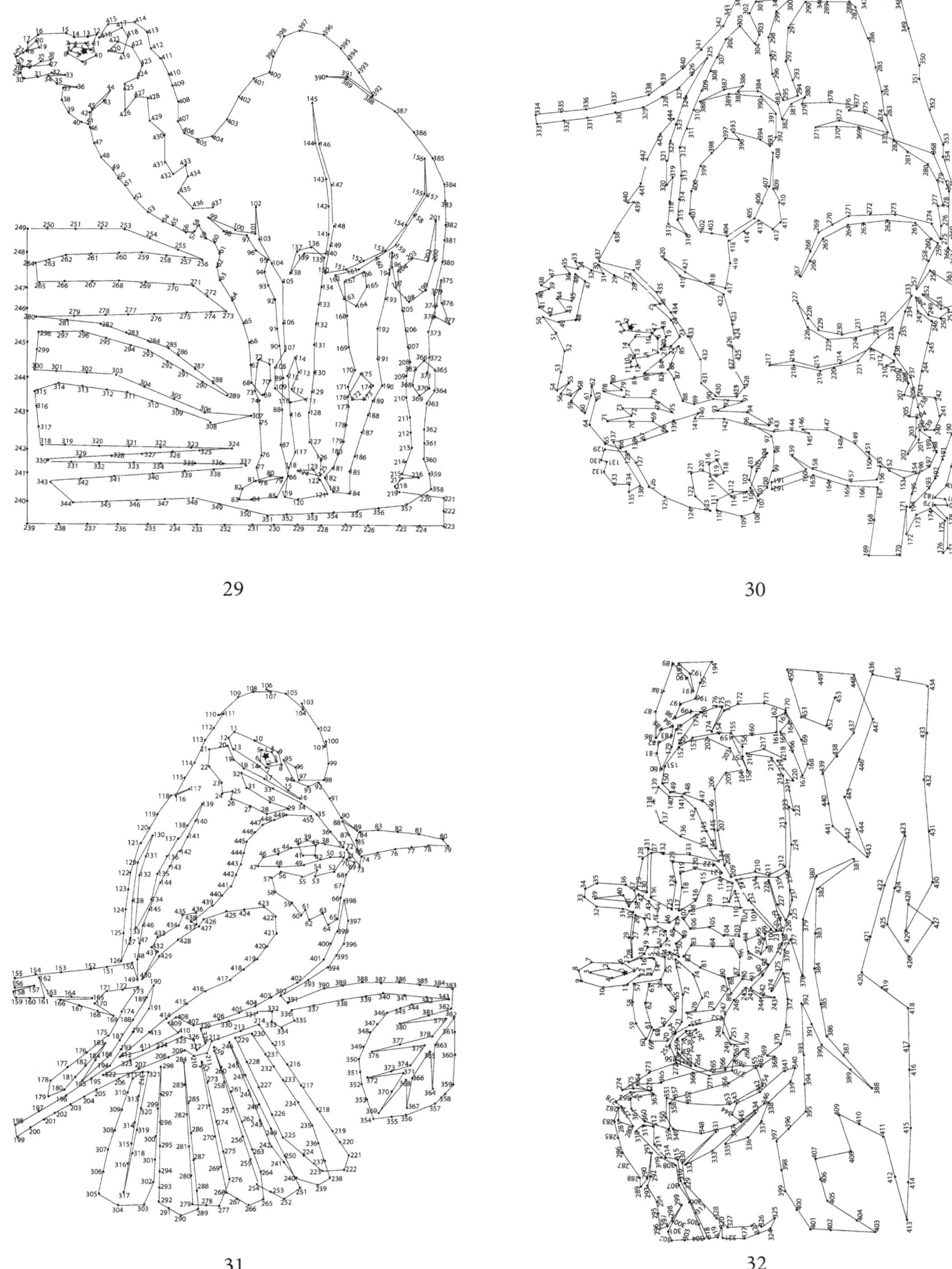

29

30

31

32

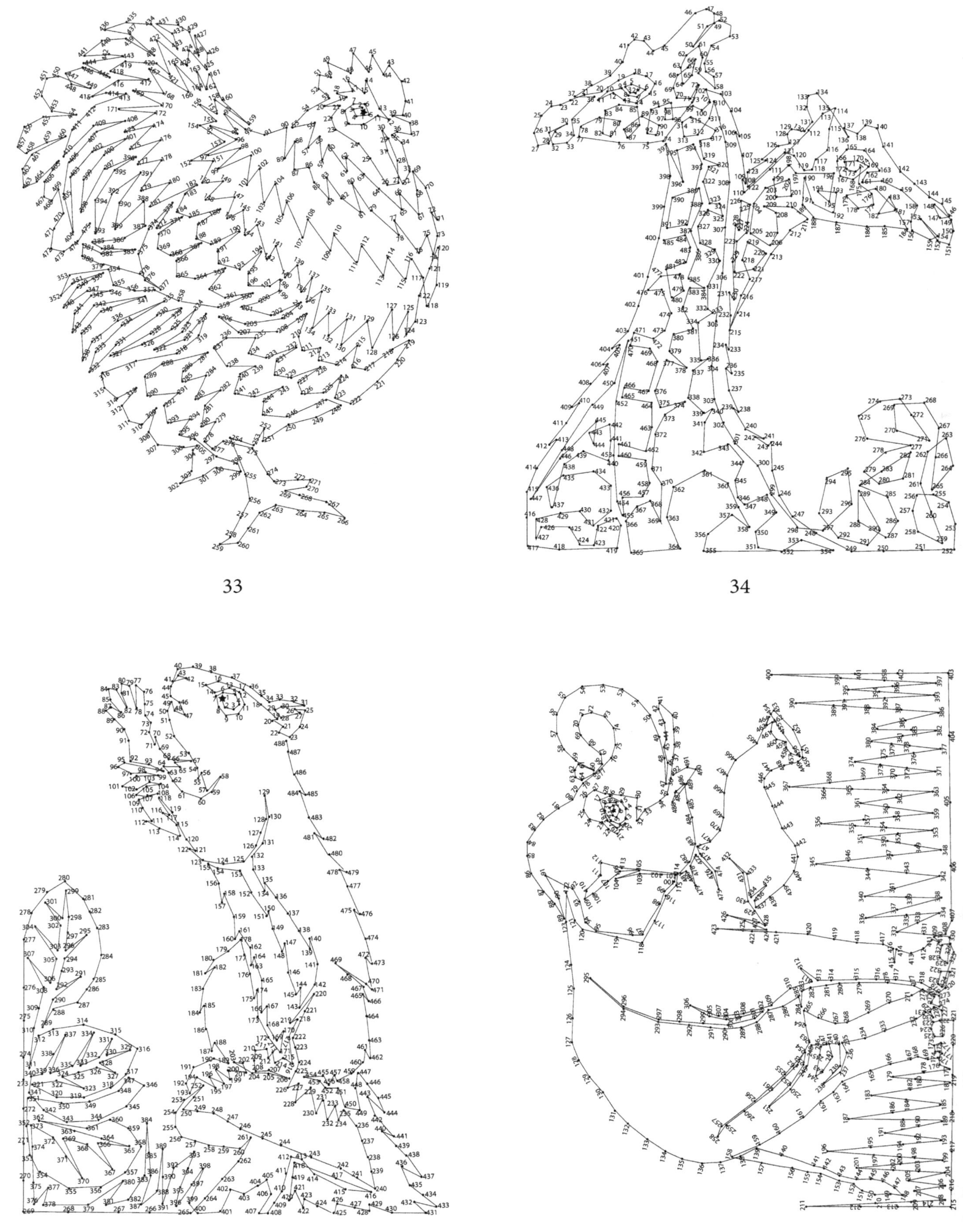

33

34

35

36

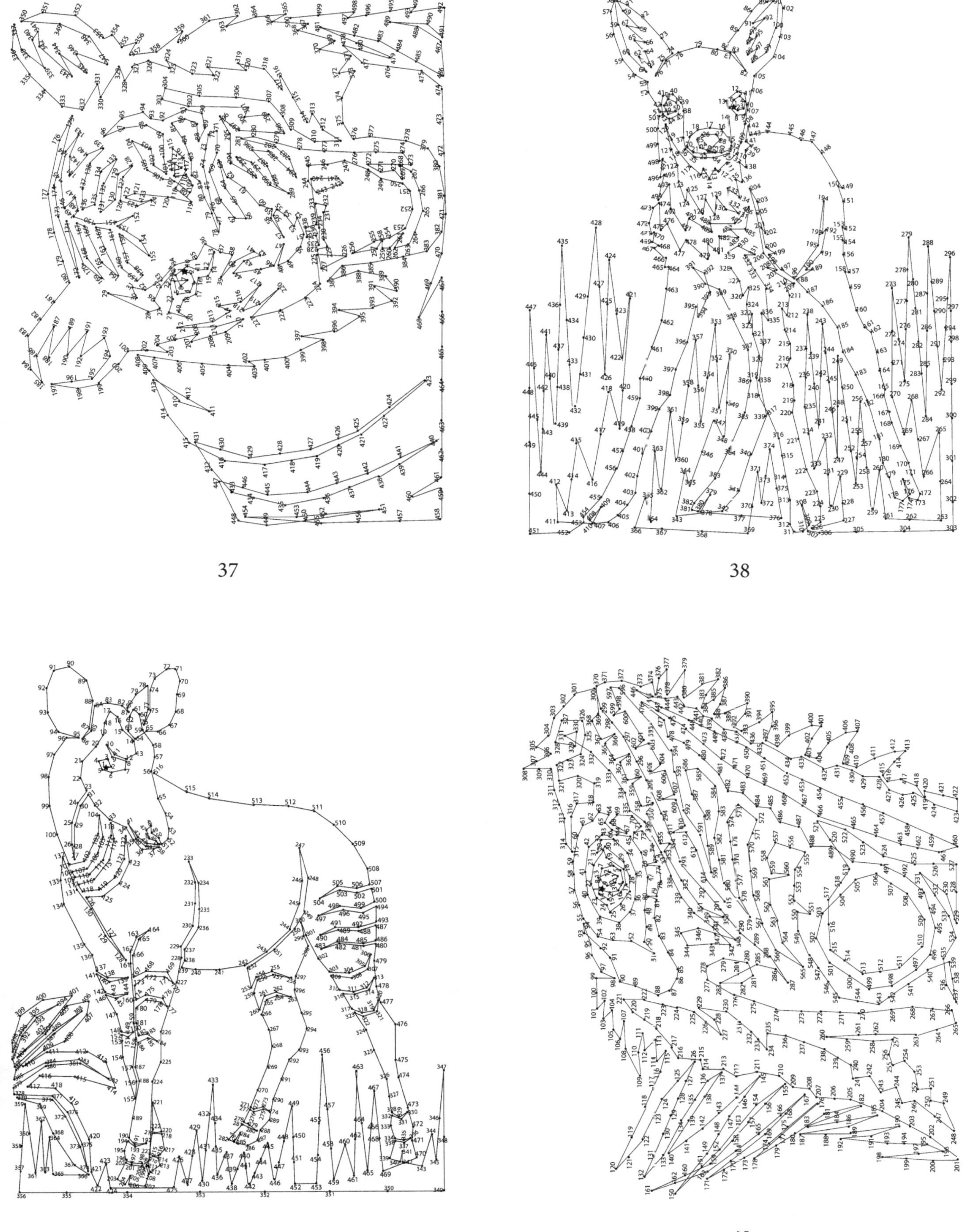

37

38

39

40

Did you know?
We Have a Great Mailing List!

Free Downloadable Dot to Dot Pages
Monthly Giveaways
Exclusive Discounts
& More!

Scan the QR Code with your phone's camera
or visit DotToDotClub.com to Join

thank you

for your purchase!
If you enjoyed this book,
please leave a review. As a
very small independent
book publisher, every
review helps us compete
with larger companies.

Scan the QR Code
to Leave a Review

(open your phone's camera
and hold it up to the
square)